Contents

KT-441-404

Plan of Book

	Topics/ Functions	Listening Skills	Grammar/ Vocabulary
Before you begin: Learn how to listen	Explaining types of listening	Listening for the main idea Listening for specific information Listening "between the lines"	
Unit 1: Meeting new people	Meeting people	Choosing appropriate responses Understanding personal information questions	Yes-no questions (present of *be* and simple present)
Unit 2: Brothers and sisters	Discussing family relationships	Understanding descriptions of people Following directions	Possessive adjectives Simple present Family words
Unit 3: Numbers	Asking for and giving (numerical) information	Understanding and processing numbers Understanding sports scores	Numbers
Unit 4: Let's eat!	Talking about food and places to eat	Inferring topics Understanding suggestions	*Let's . . .* Names of foods
Unit 5: Your free time	Talking about free-time activities	Identifying frequency Confirming and revising predictions	Frequency adverbs
Unit 6: That's a nice shirt.	Giving opinions about and describing clothing	Understanding descriptions of clothing Understanding reasons	Descriptive adjectives Clothing words
Unit 7: Furniture and houses	Describing things in a house and what they are for	Inferring topics Understanding descriptions of things	Simple present for descriptions Names of furniture and rooms in a house
Unit 8: How do you start your day?	Talking about routines	Identifying routines Understanding questions about activities	Simple present Sequence markers Simple past
Unit 9: I'd like to see that!	Giving opinions about movies	Understanding responses Inferring kinds of movies Understanding evaluations	Movie genres
Unit 10: Where is it?	Describing location and giving directions	Following directions Identifying locations	Imperatives Prepositions of location

MARC HELGESEN AND STEVEN BROWN

Active Listening

INTRODUCING

Skills for Understanding

Teacher's Edition

CAMBRIDGE
UNIVERSITY PRESS

To our parents, Ken and Esther Helgesen and Curt and Clara Brown,
who, when we were younger, often reminded us: *Listen*!

Published by the Press Syndicate of the University of Cambridge
The Pitt Building, Trumpington Street, Cambridge CB2 1RP
40 West 20th Street, New York, NY 10011-4211, USA
10 Stamford Road, Oakleigh, Melbourne 3166, Australia

First published 1995
Second printing 1996

Printed in the United States of America

Library of Congress Cataloging-in-Publication Data
has been applied for.

A catalog record for this book is available from the British Library

ISBN 0-521-39881-9   Student's Book
ISBN 0-521-39884-3   Teacher's Manual
ISBN 0-521-39887-8. Cassettes

Book design; layout and design services: Six West Design

Illustrators:
Adventure House
Daisy de Puthod
Randy Jones
Wally Neibart
Six West Design
Andrew Toos
Sam Viviano

	Topics/ Functions	Listening Skills	Grammar/ Vocabulary
Unit 11: *The Midnight Special*	Enjoying a folk song	Understanding a song Identifying a sequence of events Identifying word stress	Word stress
Unit 12: **Gifts and greetings**	Describing gifts and greetings in different countries	Identifying reasons Identifying customs	Negative imperatives (*Don't . . .*) *You shouldn't . . .*
Unit 13: **Time changes everything.**	Talking about what people did when they were younger	Identifying jobs Understanding personal information questions	Past with *used to* Names of jobs and occupations
Unit 14: **Can you describe it?**	Describing people, things, and events	Understanding descriptions of people and things Understanding descriptions of events	Descriptive adjectives
Unit 15: **Languages**	Talking about the languages of the world	Identifying countries Distinguishing types of English	American and British vocabulary and pronunciation differences
Unit 16: **I like that!**	Discussing likes and dislikes	Identifying preferences Understanding instructions	Infinitives (*to* + verb) and gerunds (verb + *-ing*)
Unit 17: **Strange news**	Evaluating newspaper headlines and stories	Understanding newspaper headlines Understanding summaries Evaluating information	Simple past
Unit 18: **Holidays**	Talking about holidays and customs in different countries	Identifying dates Identifying events	Present tenses: present of *be* and simple present for descriptions
Unit 19: **Inventions**	Describing inventions and where they came from	Understanding specific information Identifying the purpose of something	Infinitive of purpose: (*You can use it to . . .*)
Unit 20: **Folktales**	Appreciating folktales	Identifying a sequence of events Understanding and enjoying a story	Simple past

Acknowledgments

Illustrations

Adventure House   34, 36 (top), 48/49, 68/69
Daisy de Puthod   16, 24, 25, 26, 50, 60/61
Randy Jones   14, 17, 19, 23, 31, 35, 38, 39, 42, 47, 54, 65
Wally Neibart   3, 5, 10, 15, 18, 22, 29, 30, 33 (bottom), 52, 57, 58, 63, 64
Six West Design   21 (bottom), 33 (top)
Andrew Toos   4, 9, 20, 27, 36, 40, 46, 51, 62
Sam Viviano   6, 21 (top), 37, 41

Photographic credits

The authors and publisher are grateful for permission to reproduce the following photographs.

6   (*from left to right*) © The Stock Market/Roy Morsch; © The Stock Market/Michael A. Keller, 1992; © Douglas Bryant/FPG International Corp.

7   (*from top to bottom*) © Jim Cummins/FPG International Corp.; © The Stock Market/Paul Barton, 1990

13   (*clockwise from top*) © Telegraph Colour Library/FPG International Corp.; © The Stock Market/José Fuste, 1994; © James Blank/FPG International Corp.; © Russell Cheyne/Tony Stone Worldwide; © The Stock Market/Tibor Bognár, 1991; © Telegraph Colour/FPG International Corp.

28   (*clockwise from top*) © The Stock Market/Naideau, 1992; © The Stock Market/Jon Feingersh, 1989; © Telegraph Colour Library/FPG International Corp.; © J. DeSelliers/Superstock

32   (*from left to right*) © The Stock Market/Jose L. Pelaez, 1993; © P. R. Productions/Superstock

43   (*clockwise from top*) © Greg Gorman/Liaison International; © Benainous Duclos/Liaison International; © Liaison Distribution/Liaison International; © Steve Allen/Liaison International; © Steve Allen/Liaison International; © FPG International Corp.; © Frederic Reclain/Liaison International; © Kip Rano/Liaison International; © Berliner Studio/Liaison International

44   (*from left to right*) © The Stock Market/Gabe Palmer, 1990; © Ron Rovtar/FPG International Corp.; © Jade Albert/FPG International Corp.

59   (*clockwise from top*) © The Stock Market/Roy Morsch; © Telegraph Colour Library/FPG International Corp.; © Tourism Authority of Korea; © Tourism Authority of Thailand

Authors' acknowledgments

We would like to thank our **reviewers** for their helpful suggestions: Chuck Sandy and Dorolyn Smith.

We would also like to acknowledge the **students** and **teachers** in the following schools and institutes who piloted components of *Active Listening: Introducing Skills for Understanding:*

Alianza Cultural Uruguay-Estados Unidos, Montevideo, Uruguay; **Bae Centre,** Buenos Aires, Argentina; **Bunka Institute of Foreign Languages,** Tokyo, Japan; **Chin-Yi Institute of Technology,** Taichung City, Taiwan; **Educational Options,** Santa Clara, California, USA; **Impact English,** Santiago, Chile; **Instituto Cultural de Idiomas Ltda.,** Caxias do Sul, Brazil; **Kansai University of Foreign Studies,** Osaka, Japan; **Koyo Shoji Co. Ltd.,** Hitachi, Japan; **Osaka Institute of Technology,** Osaka, Japan; **Southern Illinois University,** Niigata, Japan; **Suzugamine Women's College,** Hiroshima City, Japan; **Tokyo Foreign Language College,** Tokyo, Japan; **Umeda Business College,** Osaka, Japan; **University of Michigan English Language Institute,** Ann Arbor, Michigan, USA.

Thanks also go to Hey Chang, Gerald Couzens, Betsy Davis, Marion Delarche, Carl Dusthimer, David Fisher, Yoko Futami, Robin Guenzel, Yoko Hakuta, Brenda Hayashi, Patricia Hunt, J.R. Kim, Sean Lewis, Michael McLaughlin, Susanne McLaughlin, Steven Maginn, Lalitha Manuel, Lionel Menasche, Lisa Minetti, Christine O'Neill, Ruth Owen, Susan Ryan, John Smith, Serena Spenser, Noriko Suzuki, Kazue Takahashi, Brian Tomlinson, Paul Wadden, and Michiko Wako.

Finally, a special thanks to the editors and advisors at Cambridge University Press: Suzette André, Colin Bethell, Mary Carson, Riitta da Costa, Kyoko Fukunaga, Deborah Goldblatt, John Haywood, Jinsook Kim, Stephanie Karras, Koen Van Landeghem, Kathy Niemczyk, Helen Sandiford, Kumiko Sekioka, and Mary Vaughn.

Students' introduction

Welcome to *Active Listening: Introducing Skills for Understanding*. We hope this book will help you learn to listen to English more effectively. You will practice listening to English. At the same time, you'll learn "how to listen." That is, you'll learn to make use of the English you already know. You'll also think about your reasons for listening. When you do that, listening and understanding become much easier.

This book has twenty units. Each unit has five parts:

- **Warming Up** Warming Up activities will help you remember what you know about the unit topic. This is an important step. It helps you get ready for listening.
- **Listening Task 1** You will listen to people in many different situations. Sometimes you'll listen for specific information such as numbers and places. Other times, you'll have to use what you hear to figure out things that aren't said directly. For example, you'll need to decide how strongly people feel about things they like and dislike.
- **Culture Corner** This is a short reading. It gives information about the unit topic.
- **Listening Task 2** Listening Task 2 is on the same theme as Listening Task 1, but it is a little more challenging.
- **Your Turn to Talk** This is a speaking activity. You will use the language you have just heard. You will do this task in pairs or small groups.

Listening tips

- Why are you listening? Ask yourself, "What do I need to know? What do I need to do?" You will listen to many kinds of language and do many kinds of tasks. You will need to listen in different ways. These ways are explained in the first unit, "Before You Begin." In Units 1–20, each listening task has a box at the top of the page. The box tells you the purpose of the activity.
- The tapes that go with the book are very natural. You won't be able to understand every word you hear. That's OK. You don't need to. Listen for the general meaning.
- Don't worry about words you don't know. Many students look up every new word in their dictionaries. Here's an idea: When you hear a new word, just listen. When you hear it a second time, try to guess the meaning. When you hear it a third time and still don't understand, then look it up in your dictionary.

We hope you enjoy using this book, and we hope you learn to be a better, more active listener.

Teacher's introduction

Active Listening: Introducing Skills for Understanding is a course for high-beginning to low-intermediate students of North American English. As the name implies, the course recognizes that listening is a very active process. Learners bring knowledge to the class and perform a wide variety of interactive tasks. *Active Listening* can be used as the main text for listening classes or as a supplement in speaking or integrated skills classes.

ABOUT THE BOOK

The book includes twenty units, each with a warm-up activity; two main listening tasks; Culture Corner, a reading passage that presents information related to the unit theme; and Your Turn to Talk, a short speaking activity done in pairs or small groups. In addition, there is an introductory lesson called "Before You Begin." This lesson introduces learning strategies and types of listening, including listening for gist and inference. The lesson is particularly useful for learners whose previous experience has been limited primarily to listening for specific information, or to answering literal comprehension questions.

The units can be taught in the order presented or out of sequence to follow the themes of the class or another book it is supplementing. In general, the tasks in the second half of the book are more challenging than those in the first.

Unit organization

Each unit begins with an activity called **Warming Up.** This activity, usually done in pairs, serves to remind learners of the language they already know. The tasks are designed to activate prior knowledge or "schemata." In the process of doing the warm-up activity, students work from their knowledge and, at the same time, use vocabulary and structures that are connected with a particular function or grammar point. The exercise makes the listening tasks it precedes easier because the learners are prepared.

Listening Task 1 and **Listening Task 2** are the major listening exercises. The tasks are balanced to include a variety of listening types including listening for gist, identifying specific information, and understanding inferences. The purpose of each task is identified in a box in the top-right corner of each page. Because *Active Listening* features a task-based approach, learners should be doing the activities as they listen, rather than waiting until they have finished listening to a particular segment. To make this easier, writing is kept to a minimum. In most cases, students check boxes, number items, or write only words or short phrases.

Culture Corner is a short reading passage on the theme of the unit. In most cases, you'll want to use it as homework or as a break in classroom routine. Each Culture Corner ends with one or two discussion questions.

Your Turn to Talk, the final section of each unit is a short, fluency-oriented speaking task done in pairs or small groups. In general, corrections are not appropriate during these activities. However, you may want to note common mistakes and, at the end of the period, write them on the board. Encourage learners to correct themselves.

Hints and techniques

■ Be sure to do the Warming Up section for each unit. This preview can foster a very healthy learning strategy. It teaches the students "how to listen." Also, it makes students more successful, which, in turn, motivates and encourages them.

■ In general, you'll only want to play a particular segment one or two times. If the learners are still having difficulty, try telling them the answers. Then play the tape again and let them experience understanding what they heard.

■ If some students find listening very difficult, have them do the task in pairs, helping each other as necessary. The Teacher's Edition contains additional ideas.

■ Some students may not be used to active learning. Those learners may be confused by instructions since they are used to a more passive role. Explaining activities is usually the least effective way to give instructions. It is better to demonstrate. For example, give the instruction as briefly as possible (e.g., "Listen. Number the pictures."). Then play the first part of the tape. Stop the tape and elicit the correct answer from the learners. Those who weren't sure what to do will quickly understand. The same technique works for Warming Up and Your Turn to Talk. Lead one pair or group through the first step of the task. The other learners watch. They quickly see what they are supposed to do.

Active Listening: Introducing Skills for Understanding is accompanied by a *Teacher's Edition* that contains a complete tapescript, step-by-step lesson plans, and expansion activities, as well as grammar and general notes.

FEATURES OF THE TEACHER'S EDITION

Each unit includes step-by-step lesson plans for Warming Up, Listening Task 1, Listening Task 2, and Your Turn to Talk. You'll notice that the lesson plans include "how to say it" instructions printed in *italics*. These are provided to encourage teachers to give short, direct instructions in command form since they are the easiest for learners to understand. Most lessons also offer optional steps which may be included or left out depending on the time available and the teacher's and learner's interest.

In addition to detailed teaching procedures for each activity, every unit of the Teacher's Edition also includes Notes, Additional Support activities, a Strategy Exercise, and Optional (listening/speaking) Activities.

The **Notes** include cultural information. They define idiomatic usage and provide grammatical explanations where appropriate.

The **Additional Support** activities provide another chance to listen and another purpose for listening. They may be used with classes that have a difficult time with listening.

The **Strategy Exercise** is designed to help students become more aware of their own language learning strategies and ways that they learn best. It will also make them aware that many different ways to learn exist. One important listening strategy is being aware of why one is listening. In the Strategy Exercise in Unit 3 of this Teacher's Edition, students are encouraged to listen to the tape twice. The first time, they focus on numbers. The second time, they listen for place names. Exercises such as this can help students become more aware what they are doing while they listen to and learn more English.

Strategies for learning a new language are not new. Good language learners have always used a variety of techniques to make progress. However, it is only recently that the field of English language teaching has begun to look at strategies in an organized way. Like any new aspect of teaching, strategies are promising, but they are not a magic key that will open every door.

We encourage you to look at the **Strategy Exercises** as you would any other language learning/awareness activity. Pick and choose. Select those you think would be of interest to your students. In general, encourage students to experiment with different ways to learn.

The **Optional Activities** are task-based listening/speaking activities that may be done any time during or after the completion of a unit. They give students a chance to use the language they have been hearing. A unique feature of this Teacher's Edition is the inclusion of **photocopiable activities** that are designed to be handed out to students.

HOW STUDENTS LEARN TO LISTEN

Many students find listening to be one of the most difficult skills in English. The following

---

*Thanks to Brian Tomlinson for suggesting the use of the brick-wall analogy to explain top-down/bottom-up processing.

explains some of the ideas incorporated into the book to make students more effective listeners. *Active Listening: Introducing Skills for Understanding* is designed to help students make real and rapid progress. Recent research into teaching listening and its related receptive skill, reading, have given insights into how successful students learn foreign/second languages.

Bottom-up vs. top-down processing, a brick-wall analogy

To understand what our students are going through as they learn to listen or read, consider the "bottom-up vs. top-down processing" distinction. The distinction is based on the ways learners process and attempt to understand what they read or hear. With bottom-up processing, students start with the component parts: words, grammar, and the like. Top-down processing is the opposite. Students start from their background knowledge.

This might be better understood by means of a metaphor. Imagine a brick wall. If you are standing at the bottom looking at the wall brick by brick, you can easily see the details. It is difficult, however, to get an overall view of the wall. And, if you come to a missing brick (e.g., an unknown word or unfamiliar structure), you're stuck. If, on the other hand, you're sitting on the top of the wall, you can easily see the landscape. Of course, because of distance, you'll miss some details.

Students, particularly those with years of "classroom English" but little experience in really using the language, try to listen from the "bottom up."

They attempt to piece the meaning together, word by word. It is difficult for us, as native and advanced non-native English users, to experience what learners go through. However, try reading the following *from right to left*.

> word one ,slowly English process you When to easy is it ,now doing are you as ,time a at .word individual each of meaning the catch understand to difficult very is it ,However .passage the of meaning overall the

You were probably able to understand the paragraph:

> When you process English slowly, one word at a time, as you are doing now, it is easy to catch the meaning of each individual word. However, it is very difficult to understand the overall meaning of the passage.

While reading, however, it is likely you felt the frustration of bottom-up processing; you had to get each individual part before you could make sense of it. This is similar to what our students experience – and they're having to wrestle the meaning in a foreign language. Of course, this is an ineffective way to listen since it takes too long. While students are still trying to make sense of what has been said, the speaker keeps going. The students get lost. Although their processing strategy is a negative, students do come to class with certain strengths. From their years of English study, most have a relatively large, if passive, vocabulary. They also often have a solid receptive knowledge of English grammar. We shouldn't neglect the years of life experience; our learners bring with them a wealth of background knowledge on many topics. These three strengths – vocabulary, grammar, and life experience – can be the tools for effective listening.

The Warming Up activities in *Active Listening* build on those strengths. By engaging the students in active, meaningful prelistening tasks, students integrate bottom-up and top-down processing. They start from meaning, but, in the process of doing the task, use vocabulary and structures (grammar) connected with the task, topic, or function. The result is an integrated listening strategy.

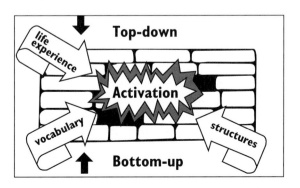

Types of listening

A second factor that is essential in creating effective listeners is exposing them to a variety of types of listening. Many students have only had experience with listening for literal comprehension. While listening for specific information is an important skill, it represents only one type. We have attempted to reach a balance in the book in order to give students experience with – and an understanding of – listening for gist and inference. Students usually are quick to understand the idea of listening for gist. They can easily imagine having to catch the general meaning of something they hear. Inference – listening "between the lines" – can be more difficult. Take the following example (from the introductory unit, "Before You Begin"). The students hear the following conversation:

Paul: Hello?
Joan: Hi, Paul. This is Joan.
Paul: Oh, hi. How are you feeling? Are you still sick?
Joan: No, I feel better, thanks. I'm going to school tomorrow. What's the homework for English class?
Paul: The homework? Just a minute. . . . OK, here it is. Read pages 23 and 24.
Joan: 23 and 24. OK. Thanks. See you tomorrow.
Paul: Bye.

Students listening for gist can easily identify "school" as the main topic of conversation, even though Joan and Paul also discuss the fact that Joan has been feeling sick. They are also able to pick out specific information, in this case, the page numbers for homework. To help learners understand the idea of inference – listening "between the lines" – ask them whether or not both students went to school today. Even though neither speaker directly says that Joan was absent, students can understand that Joan was sick and did not go to class. The key is that students understand what they are listening **for** is just as important as what they are listening **to**.

Many of these ideas are helpful in understanding the listening process, but they should not be seen as rigid models. We need to remember listening is actually very complex. A student listening for gist or inference may, for example, get the clues from catching a couple of specific bits of information.

LISTENING TRAINING TIPS

These are some helpful techniques you can try with your students so they become better listeners.

■ **Listen in pairs.** People usually think of listening as a solo skill – students do it alone even if they are in a room with lots of other learners. If a listening is challenging, try doing the task in pairs. Each pair uses only one book. That way, learners help each other by pointing out what they did understand rather than worrying about what they missed.

■ **Do something physical.** If a particular listening segment is very difficult, pick a specific item (colors, place names, etc.) that occurs four to eight times. Students close their books. Play the tape. Students do a physical action such as tapping their desks or raising their hands each time they hear the target item. The task is focused enough that most learners can accomplish it. The physical action gives immediate feedback/support to learners who missed it on the tape.

■ **Choose an appropriate level of support.** After students have heard a segment, check it as a group. Write the answers on the board. Then play the tape again. Learners choose their own level of support. Those who basically understood, close their eyes and imagine the conversations. Those who understood some, watch their books and try to hear the items mentioned. Those who found it quite challenging should watch you. As you play the tape, point to the information on the board just before it is mentioned.

■ **Listen a month later.** If your students found the natural speed of the recording very challenging at the beginning of the course, go back after a month or two. Replay a tape segment they heard earlier. They'll usually find it much easier. It helps them see their own progress.

■ **Do not look at a tapescript.** Generally, don't give students the tapescript. It reinforces word and sentence level (bottom up) processing and reinforces the myth that they can't understand meaning without catching everything they hear.

Remember that although learners need practice in listening, they also need more: They need to learn *how* to listen. They need different types of listening strategies and tasks. They need to learn to preview. Our students need exposure to it all. When learners get the exposure they need, they build their listening skills. They become active listeners.

Marc Helgesen
Steven Brown

Learn how to listen.

FROM THE PEOPLE WHO WROTE THIS BOOK

Dear students:

We hope that you learn a lot of English. We also hope that you enjoy learning it.

There are many different ways to learn. This book will help you learn to listen. Think about how you learn best. Find ways that work for you.

You need to be an active listener. When you listen, do these things:

1. Think about what you are listening <u>to</u>.
    - What is the topic?
    - What do you already know about the topic?
2. Think about what you are listening <u>for</u>.
    - What do you need to know?
    - What do you need to do?
3. When you don't understand, <u>ask</u>.
    - For example, you could say, "Could you repeat that?"

Good luck with learning English. You can do it!

Sincerely,

Marc Helgesen

Steven Brown

Learn how to listen.

Topic/function: Explaining types of listening

Listening skills: Clarifying and recognizing classroom requests (Listening Task 1); types of listening: main ideas (gist), specific information, and "between the lines" (inference) (Listening Task 2)

Note: Throughout this Teacher's Edition, the symbol "T:" followed by *italic* type indicates the teacher's script.

From the people who wrote this book

1. Hold your book so that students can see page 2. T: *Look at page 2. This is a letter from the people who wrote this book. It will help you understand "how to listen." It will also help you know how to use the book.*

2. Read the letter (or play the tape) as the students read along silently.

3. (Optional) After students have listened to the letter, have them go back and underline the most important ideas. (Answers: What are you listening to? What are you listening for? When you don't understand, ask.) OR Have them close their books. In pairs, they write what they think the most important ideas were. There is no reason the wording should be the same, only the ideas. This step can be done either in English or in their native language(s).

NOTE

• The ideas in this unit may be new to many students. As you read the letter, pause after each sentence so that students have time to think about the meaning.

Strategy exercise

Each unit of this *Teacher's Edition* introduces a language learning strategy designed to build students' awareness and control over their own learning. However, since the Before You Begin unit is entirely about listening strategies, an additional strategy is not recommended at this time.

The strategies in this unit are (a) prediction, (b) clarification, and (c) awareness of listening purpose (listening for gist, listening for specific information, understanding inferences).

Optional activities

(For use anytime during or after the unit.)

• ***Could you repeat that?*** The teacher can tell a story about something that happened recently. Students all stand. As the teacher tells the story, students interrupt the teacher using phrases from page 3. Once they have used a phrase, they can sit down. Since no one wants to be the last one standing, students will compete to interrupt. Alternatively, students can work in groups, taking turns as storyteller. Instead of standing, students in small groups can get rid of markers such as poker chips as they use the clarification phrases.

• ***Places to hear English.*** Students work in pairs for four minutes. Their task is to list as many places as they can in their city where they can hear or practice English. Once four minutes have passed, combine pairs. Which ideas were unique to a pair? Students may also set goals (Example: Which place will they visit first?) or rank the places.

Listening Task 1
Could you repeat that?

> **Listening skills:** Clarifying and recognizing classroom requests

Note: The tapescript for Before You Begin starts on page T1.

1. T: *Look at page 3.*

2. (Optional) Read the title: *"Could you repeat that?" What do you think this will be about?* Elicit answers from the students. (Answer: things to say when you want to hear something again)

3. (Optional) If your students find listening very challenging, do the Additional Support procedure.

4. Read the first set of instructions: *Work with a partner. Look at the pictures. What do you think the students are saying?* Allow time for students to work.

5. T: *Now listen. Were you correct? Write the sentences.* Play Listening Task 1 on the tape. Gesture for students to correct their answers.

6. (Optional) To make sure students understand what to do, stop after the first item and check. Ask: *What is "E – M"?* (Answer: Excuse me?) Then play the rest of Listening Task 1.

7. If necessary, play Listening Task 1 a second time.

8. Check by eliciting answers from the students. Write them on the board. (Answers appear in blue on the opposite page.)

9. Follow up by having students close their books. In pairs, they try to remember and say each sentence. OR Have students close their books. Play the tape again. Students raise their hands each time they hear a clarification phrase. (Raising their hands keeps students involved, gives you feedback as to what they notice, and cues weaker students who can "see the answers" as others raise their hands.)

ADDITIONAL SUPPORT Most students will already know many clarification phrases. Give one or two examples, then have them work in groups of three or four. They see how many clarification phrases they can write in five minutes. Then have them call out their ideas. Write the phrases on the board.

NOTES

• Make a poster of the phrases on page 3. You can direct the students' attention to the poster when they need help with feedback language.

• Most students have previously learned these simple patterns. Many, however, are not used to using them. The book begins with this activity to remind students that it is their responsibility to ask for clarification.

• Students predict what the people in the pictures are saying both to get practice with a useful strategy (prediction) and to help them identify their mistakes.

• Some students may be surprised to see "Excuse me?" listed for clarification. This is because they learned it as a pattern to be used when apologizing for mistakes (meaning, "I'm sorry") or for interrupting (Example: Excuse me. Can I ask a question?). "Excuse me?" as a question is usually used to ask someone to repeat something.

• In the cartoon, the teacher is speaking too rapidly without pausing, and this creates the confusion. She is actually saying, "Open your books to page 18."

Could you repeat that?

❑ Work with a partner.
Look at the pictures.
What do you think the students are saying?

❑ Now listen. Were you correct?
Write the sentences.

What do you say when . . .

1. you want someone to say something again?

Open your books to page 18.

C<u>ould you</u> r<u>epeat</u> that?

E <u>xcuse</u> m<u>e</u> ?

2. you want to hear the tape again?

Once m<u>ore</u> , p<u>lease</u> .

3. you don't know how to spell a word?

H<u>ow</u> d<u>o</u> <u>you</u> spell (that)?

4. you want to know a word in English?

H<u>ow</u> d<u>o</u> <u>you</u> say (that) in English?

3

Types of listening

There are many ways to listen. We listen differently for different reasons.

1 **Listening for the main idea**
Listen to the conversation.
What is the most important idea? Check (✔) your answer.

 ✔ dinner   ☐ a movie   ☐ school

Sometimes you don't need to understand everything you hear. You just want the general meaning.

2 **Listening for specific information**
Listen again.
What are they going to eat? Check (✔) your answer.

☐ hamburgers   ✔ pizza   ☐ spaghetti

Sometimes you only need to understand certain information. Ask yourself, "What am I listening for?"

3 **Listening "between the lines"**
Listen again.
Will they go together? Check (✔) your answer.

✔ Yes   ☐ No

Sometimes people don't say the exact words. You can still understand the meaning.

Listening Task 2
Types of listening

> **Listening skills:** Listening for main ideas (gist), listening for specific information, listening "between the lines" (inference)

1. T: *Look at page 4.*

2. (Optional) Read the title: *"Types of listening." What do you think this will be about?* Elicit answers from the students. (Answer: listening purposes)

3. (Optional) If your students find listening very challenging, do the Additional Support procedure.

4. Read the instructions: *There are many ways to listen. We listen differently for different reasons. Number 1. Listening for the main idea. Listen to the conversation. What is the most important idea? Check your answer.*

5. Play the first item on the tape. Gesture for students to check their answers.

6. (Optional) To make sure students understand what to do, stop after the first item. T: *The main idea is "dinner." You didn't understand everything. You didn't need to. You only needed to understand the main idea.*

7. Continue with the second item in the same way. After students have marked their answer, elicit it from them. (Answer: pizza)

8. Continue with the third item the same way you did 1 and 2. (Answer: yes)

9. (Optional) Since the idea of listening "between the lines" may be new to some students, it is useful to stop after number 3. T: *Yes, they're going together. But they never say, "Yes, let's go." How did you know?* Elicit answers. (Answers: The man says, "Maybe," then "I love pizza!")

10. Do the second task (page 5) in the same way. To help students get used to dealing with longer segments, different tasks, and quick responses, play all three items without stopping.

11. Check by eliciting answers. Write them on the board. (Answers appear in blue on pages 4 and 5.)

12. Read the conclusion. T: *You heard the same conversation three times. Each time, you listened for different reasons. Always think about why you are listening.*

13. You may want to play the tape again. If you do, point to the answers on the board just before they are said on the tape. This helps weaker students.

ADDITIONAL SUPPORT Have students work in pairs. They look at all six pictures on page 4. Next to each picture, they write a specific example. For the top three pictures, they should write the name of a restaurant, a movie theater, and a school they all know. For the second set of pictures, they should write restaurants where they can find each of the foods listed.

NOTES

• Students may be surprised to hear the same tape segment used for all three parts of the task. However, for most students, it clearly illustrates how the reason for listening (the task) is different, even with the same bit of language.

• The labels for types of listening (listening for the main idea, listening for specific information, listening "between the lines") are fairly technical. We have limited the number of such words taught in the book. However, having students know a few key words can help focus their learning. Having students know these words also makes it easier for you as the teacher to direct students' attention to the purpose of each task.

• "Listening for the main idea" is also called "listening for gist" or "global listening."

Listening Task 2 *(cont.)*

See page 4 for the procedure for the listening activities on this page.

NOTES *(cont.)*

• "Listening for specific information" is also called "listening for details" and "focused listening." It is useful for students to understand that listening for specific information does not mean understanding every word and picking out the information they need. Rather, it involves understanding the task and focusing on it to catch that particular information.

• "Listening 'between the lines'" is also called "understanding inferences." It is often the most challenging for learners, both because it is abstract and because students have little experience with it. Assure the students that they will be given plenty of practice with all the types of listening in this book.

• If students have difficulty understanding the concept of "listening between the lines," try the following. Write these sentences on the board:

1. Bring the phone to the bathroom.
2. You answer it.
3. I want to call someone.

Read the following:
Listen. What does B mean?
A: The phone's ringing.
B: I'm taking a bath.

Elicit answers from the choices on the board. (The answer is 2. [You answer it.] B means that A should answer the phone.) This example can help students understand that inference (listening between the lines) is not just imagining meaning. It is thinking about meaning that is given, even though the specific words aren't used.

Your turn to talk

Because this is the first unit, no Your Turn to Talk appears. The authors felt it was important to keep the unit as clear and simple as possible, especially since the concepts are new to many learners. However, an Optional Activity appears below for classes where time and level make expansion practical.

Optional activity

(For use anytime during or after the unit.)

• *What did you say?* Brainstorm clarification phrases. If practical, it can be useful to give each group a large piece of paper and a magic marker so they can write in large letters. After they've written their phrases, groups exchange papers. They note any sentences they hadn't written. They also correct any grammar or spelling mistakes they can. Next, they call out the sentences, which you write on the board. Finally, in their groups, they take turns "lip-reading" a sentence (that is, they form words with their mouths without making any sound). Partners watch and try to be the first to say the same sentence aloud.

Try it again. Two friends are talking on the telephone.
Each time you listen, think about the information you need.

1 Listening for the main idea
Listen. What is the most important idea?
Check (✔) your answer.

☐ going to the doctor   ✔ school

2 Listening for specific information
Listen. Which page numbers should she read?
Write the page numbers.

___23___ and ___24___

3 Listening "between the lines"
Listen again. Did both students go to school today?
Check (✔) your answer.

☐ Yes   ✔ No

You heard the same conversation three times.
Each time, you listened for different reasons.
Always think about why you are listening.

5

Meeting new people

WARMING
UP

❏ Work with a partner.
  Tell your partner about yourself.
  Where are you from? What do you do?
  What do you like?

> I'm Ruth. I'm from Taipei. I'm a teacher.

> I'm Charles. I'm from Montreal. I like jazz.

> I'm Marta. I'm from Mexico City. I like to read.

SAMPLE
ANSWERS

I'm _____*Koji*_____ .

I'm from _____*Tokyo*_____ .

I'm a _____*student*_____ .

I like _____*movies*_____ .

I don't like _____*sports*_____ .

U N I T   1
Meeting new people

> ***Topic/function:*** Meeting people
> ***Listening skills:*** Choosing appropriate responses (Listening Task 1); understanding personal information questions (Listening Task 2)
> ***Grammar/vocabulary:*** Yes-no questions (present of *be* and simple present)

Warming Up

1. Hold your book so that students can see page 6. T: *Look at page 6.*

2. Read the instructions. Pause when you see the symbol ♦ to give students time to answer the questions.

> *Work with a partner.*
> *Tell your partner about yourself.*
> *Where are you from? What do you do?*
> *What do you like?* ♦

3. Allow students time to introduce themselves.

4. (Optional) Have students stand and circulate. They should introduce themselves to as many people as possible in five minutes.

NOTE

• The purpose of Warming Up is to "activate" (remind the students of) words, grammar, and content they have already learned. In most cases, mistakes in grammar should be ignored at this time unless they make understanding difficult. It is better to simply repeat the sentence correctly. Students will be hearing correct models many times during the unit.

Strategy exercise: *Recognizing and using common patterns*

Every language is full of set phrases and common patterns (routines). One way to become a better listener is to anticipate

and recognize these patterns. If a listening activity is about introductions and meeting people, we expect to hear, "Hello, I'm Sue. I'm from New York." and "John, this is Mary. Mary, John. Mary is in my English class." Learning to anticipate these set phrases can decrease the work necessary when listening. Knowing which phrases are likely to be used allows students to get ready for the information they need. To get this point across, before listening to Listening Task 1, tell the students they are going to hear people introduce themselves at a party. Ask them what people say to introduce themselves in English and in their language(s). Write the guesses on the board.

Optional activities

(For use anytime during or after the unit.)

• ***Things in common.*** Students work in pairs. They try to find three things that they have in common. You might want to brainstorm a list of possible questions on the board before you begin the pair work (Are you from this city/town? Do you like jazz?, etc.). After the pair work, students introduce their partner to another pair.

• ***Pantomime introductions.*** Begin by brainstorming the kinds of things people talk about when they first meet (where they live, jobs, interests, families, movies, etc.). Students then work in pairs or groups of three. One person pantomimes information about him/herself. The partners guess what it means.

• ***I'm Madonna.*** Students choose a famous person they would like to be. They work in pairs to have dialogs like those in Listening Task 1, introducing themselves as the famous person they have chosen.

Listening Task 1 Hello!

Note: The tapescript for Unit 1 begins on page T3.

1. T: *Look at page 7.*

2. (Optional) Read the title: *"Hello!" What do you think this will be about?* Elicit answers from the students. (Answer: meeting people)

3. (Optional) If your students find listening very challenging, do the Additional Support procedure below.

4. Read the instructions: *You're at a party. You're meeting Kent and Lisa for the first time. Listen to Kent. What is your part of the conversation? Check your answers.*

5. Play the first part of the tape. Gesture for students to check their answers.

6. (Optional) To make sure students understand what to do, stop after number two. Ask students: *What did you check?* (Answer: I like it, too.) Then play the rest of Step One.

7. Read the instructions to Step Two: *Listen. Now you are talking to Lisa. What is your part of this conversation? Check your answers.*

8. Play Step Two. Gesture for students to check their answers.

9. If necessary, play Listening Task 1 a second time.

10. Check by having students read the sentences they checked. (Answers appear in blue on the opposite page.)

ADDITIONAL SUPPORT Have students work in pairs. They look at the answers in Part One ("Yes, I'll have orange juice" through "I really like this music") Tell them they will hear people talking at a party. They should write a question they might hear for each answer (Example:

Would you like something to drink? Do you want something to eat?, etc.).

Note that there are many different ways to say something. It doesn't matter if the students' predictions are "correct" – the ones actually used on the tape. By doing the activity, they are becoming familiar with the content and vocabulary they'll need to do the task.

NOTES

• You may want to include students speaking in this activity either by having students say their answers instead of checking them or by having them do the activity orally after they have completed the checking task. In that case, you might want to have them close their books and use their own ideas for the questions about music and something to drink.

• This listening task presents a common North American party conversation. Typically, people circulate and talk to each other for short periods of time. Topics of conversation include music and food and drink. People generally speak for a short time before introducing themselves.

• "Club soda" is carbonated water.

Culture corner

Culture Corner is a short reading passage which appears at the bottom of each Listening Task 1 page. An optional activity for using the Culture Corner passage is given in every unit of this *Teacher's Edition*.

1. After students have read the Culture Corner, have them answer this question in pairs or small groups: *Are these topics good things to talk about in your country?*

2. (Optional) Before students have read the Culture Corner, have them work in groups of three. They list topics to talk about when they first meet someone. They should see how many they can list in three minutes. Then they read the Culture Corner to see if the topics they wrote are mentioned.

Hello!

You're at a party.
You're meeting Kent and Lisa for the first time.

Kent

❏ **Listen to Kent.**
What is your part of the conversation?
Check (✔) your answers.

1. ☑ Yes, I'll have orange juice.
   ☐ I'm hungry.

2. ☐ Yes. The orange juice is very good.
   ☑ I like it, too.

3. ☐ Nice to meet you. I am too.
   ☑ Nice to meet you. I'm *(your name)*.

4. ☑ I'm a *(your job)*.
   ☐ I really like this music.

Lisa

❏ **Listen. Now you are talking to Lisa.**
What is your part of this conversation?
Check (✔) your answers.

1. ☑ Yes, I'm having fun.
   ☐ I'm hungry.

2. ☐ Nice to meet you. I am too.
   ☑ Nice to meet you. I'm *(your name)*.

3. ☐ Yes, the music is really good.
   ☑ I'm from *(your hometown)*.

4. ☑ Yes, club soda, please.
   ☐ I like it, too.

CULTURE CORNER

In the United States and Canada, people talk about these things when they meet for the first time:

- the place where they are ("This is a great party.")
- the weather ("Nice day, isn't it?")
- something that is the same for both people ("I live on Oak Street, too.")

Are these topics good things to talk about in your country?

7

Do you . . . ? Are you . . . ?

❑ Listen. Finish the sentences.

❑ Are these sentences true for you? Circle "yes" or "no."

PERSONAL SURVEY

1. Do you like jazz_____?   Yes   No

2. Are you from a *small_____ town_____*?   Yes   No

3. Do you like *tennis_____*?   Yes   No

4. Do you like *fish_____*?   Yes   No

5. Are you from a *big_____ family_____*?   Yes   No

6. Do you like *dogs_____*?   Yes   No

7. Are you a *new_____ student_____*?   Yes   No

8. Do you *like_____ English_____*?   Yes   No

YOUR TURN TO TALK

Find someone who. Stand up. Find a partner. Ask one of the questions above. When your partner says "No," ask a different question. When your partner says "Yes," write the person's name next to the question. Then change partners.

Examples

A: Do you like jazz?   A: Are you from a . . . ?
B: Yes, I do. *(Write B's name.)* C: No, I'm not.
                                   A: Do you like . . . ?

Listening Task 2
Do you . . . ? Are you . . . ?

> **Listening skill:** Understanding personal information questions

1. T: *Look at page 8.*

2. (Optional) Read the title: *"Do you . . . ? Are you . . . ?" What do you think this will be about?* Elicit answers from the students. (Answer: personal information)

3. (Optional) If your students find listening very challenging, do the Additional Support procedure.

4. Read the first part of the instructions: *Listen. Finish the sentences.*

5. Play Listening Task 2 on the tape. Gesture for students to write the missing words.

6. (Optional) To make sure students understand what to do, stop after the second item. Ask students: *What did you write?* (Answer: small town) Then play the rest of Listening Task 2.

7. If necessary, play Listening Task 2 a second time. Before replaying the tape, you may want to have students compare their answers to the dictation part of the activity: *Work with a partner. Look at the words your partner wrote. Were they the same as your answers? Then we'll listen again.*

8. Check by having students call out what they wrote. (Answers appear in blue on the opposite page.)

9. Read the second part of the instructions: *Are these sentences true for you? Circle "yes" or "no."* Make sure that students understand that the Yes/No section uses their own information, not something on the tape. Gesture for them to circle "yes" or "no."

10. Have students raise their hands to indicate their answers. **Note:** If you are going to do the Your Turn to Talk activity ("Find someone who"), do not ask how many students circled yes/no at this time.

ADDITIONAL SUPPORT Have students close their books. Play the tape once. In pairs, they try to catch the last two words of each question. This will help them focus on the content words they'll need to do the task.

NOTE

• Don't worry about the definitions of "small town" and "big family." Let the students decide the sizes for themselves.

Your turn to talk

Note: This is a version of the classic activity "Find someone who."

1. Read the instructions: *Find someone who. Stand up. Find a partner. Ask one of the questions above. When your partner says "No," ask a different question. When your partner says "Yes," write the person's name next to the question. Then change partners.*

2. Demonstrate the activity by walking up to one student (as all the other students watch). T: *Do you like jazz?* If the answer is "Yes," write the student's name next to the item. If the answer is "No," ask a different question. Continue until you find a question with a "Yes" answer. Then change partners.

3. T: *Stand up. Ask the questions. Try to find one person for each question.*

NOTE

• "Find someone who" works best when students are standing and moving around since they need to talk to many people. If the classroom makes movement impossible (which is rare – even in a crowded language lab, students can talk over the booths), the activity can be done in pairs as a simple match game. Students ask the questions and see how many times they and their partners gave the same answer.

Brothers and sisters

Topic/function: Discussing family
relationships
Listening skills: Understanding descriptions
of people (Listening Task 1); following
directions (Listening Task 2)
Grammar/vocabulary: Possessive adjectives,
simple present, family words

Warming Up

1. Hold your book so that students can see
page 9. T: *Look at page 9.*

2. Read the instructions. Pause when you
see the symbol ♦ to give students time to
answer the questions.

> *Work with a partner.*
> *Look at the family tree.*
> *How are these people related?*
> *Write the numbers in the circles.* ♦

3. As students work, circulate and help
pairs having difficulty. If there are terms
students don't know, encourage them to
skip those items and come back to them
later.

4. Check by reading the names of the
characters. Elicit the answers from the
students. T: *Jack and Carrie are husband and
wife. What are Kathleen and Billy?* etc.
(Answers appear in blue on the opposite
page.)

NOTES

• For a challenge, have students cover up
the vocabulary at the top of the page. They
can see how many words they already know
before they complete the task.

• Unlike some languages, English has no
separate nouns to indicate birth order.
Instead "older (or elder)" and "younger"
are used to explain relationships: "He's my
older brother."

• Generations before grandparents are
identified with the word "great." Your
grandparents' mother and father are your
"great-grandparents." Their parents are
your "great-great-grandparents," etc.

Strategy exercise: *Associating*

People learn by associating new
information with old. Often, students are
not as successful as they could be because
they see English as a random collection of
rules and words. Divide students into
groups of four or five. Give all groups the
same word and set a time limit. One
student in each group is the secretary. The
groups race against each other to list as
many associated words as they can. The
group with the most associations wins.
Family words are good examples because
they fall naturally into groups and students
have a lot of associations with them. Once
students understand associating, you can
choose words from other areas.

Optional activity

(For use anytime during or after the unit.)

• *Me too!* Have the students stand up.
They walk around the room trying to find
one thing that is the same about their
family and their partner's family. It can be
whatever students choose, and it can
change with partners (number of brothers,
ages, likes and dislikes, etc.). Once they
find something in common, they should
move on and talk to other students and try
to find things in common with them.

Variation: The thing in common doesn't
change. Once they find a partner with that
thing in common, the two students should
go together to find a third, a fourth, and
so on. The group that grows largest
quickest is the winner.

Brothers and sisters

❏ Work with a partner.
Look at the family tree.
How are these people related?
Write the numbers in the circles.

1. husband • wife
2. mother • son
3. father • daughter
4. brother • sister
5. aunt • nephew
6. uncle • niece
7. grandfather • granddaughter
8. grandmother • grandson
9. father-in-law • daughter-in-law
10. brother-in-law • sister-in-law

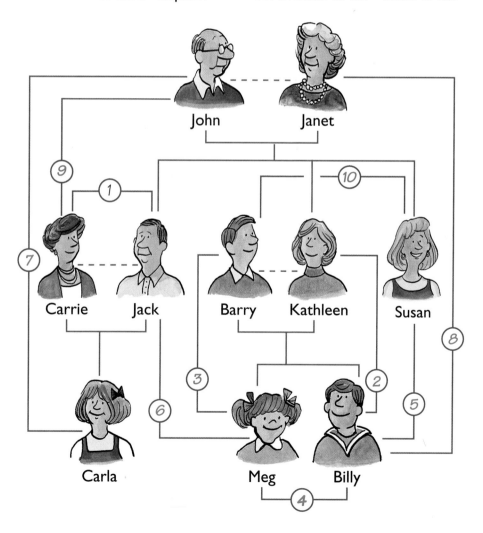

Family snapshots

❑ Listen. People are talking about their families.
Which are the correct pictures?
Check (✔) your answers.

 1.

 2.

3.

4.

The word "family" means different things in different countries. In some
countries, grandparents live with the family. In other places, only children and
parents live together. In some countries, children live with their parents until
they get married. In others, young people leave their parents' home after high
school. Here are average family sizes:

Egypt	4.9 people	Germany	2.3
Korea	4.1	The United States	2.6
New Zealand	3.0		

Who lives together in your country? Do you have a large family?

10

Listening Task 1
Family snapshots

> **Listening skill:** Understanding descriptions of people

Note: The tapescript for Unit 2 begins on page T4.

1. T: *Look at page 10.*

2. (Optional) Read the title: "*Family snapshots.*" *What do you think this will be about?* Elicit answers from the students. (Answer: pictures of families)

3. (Optional) If your students find listening very challenging, do the Additional Support procedure below.

4. Read the instructions: *Listen. People are talking about their families. Which are the correct pictures? Check your answers.*

5. Play Listening Task 1 on the tape. Gesture for students to check their answers.

6. (Optional) To make sure students understand what to do, stop after one or two items. Ask students: *Which picture, the top one or the bottom one? How did you know?* Elicit answers. Then play the rest of Listening Task 1.

7. If necessary, play Listening Task 1 a second time.

8. Check by eliciting answers from the students. It is also useful to elicit how they knew. This is especially important so those who missed some items can hear the clues that helped the other students. (Answers appear in blue on the opposite page.)

ADDITIONAL SUPPORT Have students work in pairs. Tell them that they will hear parents describing their families. They should look at the pictures and identify what they think the relationships are between family members (mother • daughter, etc.). Also, they can guess either the ages of the people or the types of schools (elementary, junior high, etc.) that the children in the pictures attend.

Culture corner

1. After students have read the Culture Corner, have them answer the questions in pairs or small groups: *Who lives together in your country? Do you have a large family?*

2. (Optional) Before students read the Culture Corner, write the following lists on the chalkboard:

- Egypt, Germany, Korea, New Zealand, The United States
- 2.3 people, 2.6, 3.0, 4.1, 4.9

Tell the students the numbers indicate the average family size in these countries, but they are in the wrong order. Students write the names of the countries and guess which number goes with each country. They then read to see if they were right.

Note: Students should understand that they are just guessing and that this isn't a test. There is no way they could be expected to know the correct answers. However, by guessing, many students become more interested in reading to see if they were right.

Optional activity

- *My pictures.* Have students bring pictures of their own families. In pairs, show the pictures and say as much as possible about each person. Another option is to show the picture and tell about it, making a few "mistakes" (e.g., saying a brother is "60" instead of "16," identifying one's father as "mother," etc.) Partners listen and try to catch the mistakes. If students have several pictures, they can show them all. They describe one picture, and the partner has to identify it.

Listening Task 2
Your family tree

Listening skill: Following directions

1. T: *Look at page 11.*

2. (Optional) Read the title: *"Your family tree."* *What do you think this will be about?* Elicit answers from the students. (Answer: the students' own families)

3. (Optional) If your students find listening very challenging, do the Additional Support procedure below.

4. Read the instructions: *You're going to write about your family. You need to know these shapes: star, square, diamond, circle.* (Point to the shapes in your book or draw them on the board.)

5. T: *Listen. Write your answers.* Play Listening Task 2 on the tape. Gesture for students to write information about themselves in the correct shapes.

6. (Optional) To make sure students understand they are really writing about themselves, stop after the first item. Draw a star on the board. Ask: *What was number one?* Elicit the answer (name and birthday). Write the information for yourself as a model. Then play the rest of Listening Task 2.

7. If necessary, play Listening Task 2 a second time.

8. Check by asking what kind of information goes in each shape. T: *Whose name did you write in the square? What else did you write?* etc. (Answers appear in blue on the opposite page.)

ADDITIONAL SUPPORT Have students close their books. They listen once and raise their hands anytime they hear a family relationship word.

Variation: Write *when, where, how* on the chalkboard. As students listen, they raise their hand when they hear family relationship words and when they hear "when," "where," or "how."

NOTES

• You may prefer to check answers after each segment rather than waiting until students have heard all four parts.

• This activity is related to TPR (Total Physical Response). In TPR, students follow directions from the teacher or a tape. In this case, the directions are about where to write personal information. It is rather unusual in a listening book to have the tape "talk directly to the students" (as opposed to having students overhear conversations.) Make sure they understand that the tape is talking to them and they should write personal information based on the directions.

Your turn to talk

1. Divide the class into groups of three. T: *Take turns. Tell about the people in your family. Say at least three sentences about each person.*

2. (Optional) Give an example about yourself. T: *My mother lives in _____. She's a (job). She likes to _____.*

NOTE

• You may want to have partners look at the speaker's family tree from Listening Task 2 as they do the activity. This not only gives the partners a visual prompt, it also means they are looking at something other than the speaker. That can help make the speaker less nervous about a spontaneous "mini-speech" in English.

Optional activity

(For use anytime during or after the unit.)

• *Who is it?* After students work together in Your Turn to Talk, have them work in the same groups to guess which family members their partners are describing.

Your family tree

You're going to write about your family. You need to know these shapes:

star = ☆   square = ☐   diamond = ◇   circle = ○

❏ Listen. Write your answers.

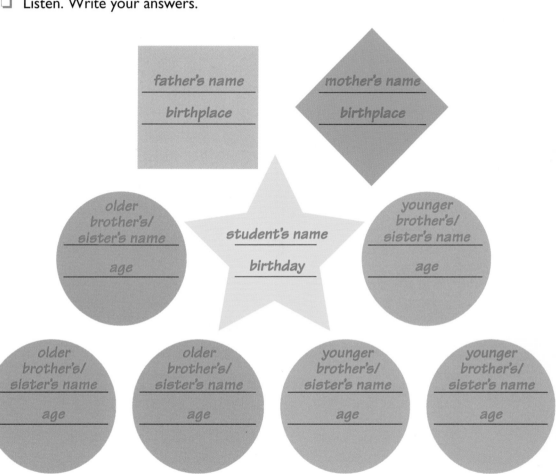

father's name
birthplace

mother's name
birthplace

older brother's/ sister's name
age

student's name
birthday

younger brother's/ sister's name
age

older brother's/ sister's name
age

older brother's/ sister's name
age

younger brother's/ sister's name
age

younger brother's/ sister's name
age

YOUR TURN TO TALK

Work in groups of three. Take turns. Tell about the people in your family. Say at least three sentences about each person:

- Where do they live?
- What kind of work do they do?
- What do they do in their free time?

- What do they look like?
- Why do you like them?

Example: My sister lives in Australia. She's a doctor. She plays tennis in her free time. . . .

11

Numbers

WARMING UP

❏ Work with a partner.
Who can count to 100 in English faster?
Begin at the same time. Count as fast as you can. Who won?

❏ Now play the number game. Follow the instructions below.

THE NUMBER GAME

Say these numbers: *SAMPLE ANSWERS*
- your birthday *6/27/74*
- your phone number *855-8130*
- your address *93 Pine Street*
- an important date *May 23*

Partner, listen and cross out (X) each number you hear. Take turns.

X̶	X̶	X̶	X̶	4	X̶	X̶	7	X̶
9	10	11	12	13	14	15	16	17
18	19	20	21	22	X̶3̶	24	25	26
27	28	29	30	31	32	33	34	35
36	37	38	39	40	41	42	43	44
45	46	47	48	49	50	51	52	53
54	55	56	57	58	59	60	61	62
63	64	65	66	67	68	69	70	71
72	73	X̶4̶	75	76	77	78	79	80
81	82	83	84	85				
86	87	88	89	90				
91	92	X̶3̶	94	95				
96	97	98	99	100				

Did your partner cross out the correct numbers?
Each correct number = 1 point.

Your points: _____

Numbers

Topic/function: Asking for and giving
(numerical) information
Listening skills: Understanding and
processing numbers (Listening Task 1);
understanding sports scores (Listening
Task 2)
Grammar/vocabulary: Numbers

Warming Up

1. Hold your book so that students can see page 12. T: *Look at page 12. This lesson is about numbers.*

2. Read the instructions. Pause when you see the symbol ♦ to give students time to answer the questions.

> *Work with a partner.*
> *Who can count to 100 in English faster?*
> *Begin at the same time. Count as fast as*
>   *you can.* ♦

3. Continue with the script:

> *Who won? Now play the number game.*
>   *Follow the instructions below.*
> *Say these numbers: Your birthday, your phone*
>   *number, your address, an important date.*
> *Partner, listen and cross out each number you*
>   *hear. Take turns.* ♦

4. Demonstrate by having one pair start the activity while other students watch. Ask one student: *When is your birthday?* Repeat the answer and have the partner cross out the numbers (month, date, and year [if given]). Then say: *See how many numbers you can cross out.*

5. (Optional) After some pairs have finished the four items given, have them continue: *Keep going. You can use any numbers: your age, the age of people in your family, a student number, anything. Say the number and what it means. Partner, cross it out. How many different numbers can you cross out?*

6. When the students have finished, say: *Count the numbers you crossed out. You get one point for each. How many points?* Elicit totals.

NOTES

•   This activity can be done as a cooperative game by having each pair use only one book. They both cross out numbers on the same number grid. Include the activity expansion in Step 5. They see how many numbers they can cross out together.

•   In the game, longer numbers can be used in parts. For example, if a student was born in 1978, that number could be used for 1-9-7-8, 19-78, 1-97-8, etc.

•   Most students have already learned numbers in English. However, they often haven't had enough practice using them. This unit gives enough practice so students can use numbers fluently.

Strategy exercise: *Focusing on specific words*

It is sometimes useful for students to anticipate and listen for specific words that contain the information they need. In this unit, they are listening for numbers and should be encouraged to focus on that information. After students listen for the numbers in Listening Task 1, play the tape again. This time, have them listen for place names. Ask them to notice how the task changed.

Optional activity

(For use anytime during or after the unit.)

•   *Number race.* Students stand and face their partners. They hold their hands out in front of them. They count to 100 as fast as they can. Each student in a pair says every other number: (A: 1, B: 2, A: 3, B: 4, etc.). Each time they say a number, they gently slap their partner's hands. When you say *Go!* they race to 100.

Once they understand the activity, have them continue, then count in various ways (By 3's [3, 6, 9, 12, etc.], by 7's, by 9's, etc.).

Listening Task 1
Information

> **Listening skill:** Understanding and processing numbers

Note: The tapescript for Unit 3 begins on page T5.

1. T: *Look at page 13.*

2. (Optional) Read the title: *"Information."* *What do you think this will be about?* Elicit answers from the students. (Answer: asking for telephone numbers)

3. (Optional) If your students find listening very challenging, do the Additional Support procedure below.

4. Read the instructions: *Listen. People want to know the telephone numbers for places in these cities. Write the telephone numbers.*

5. Play Listening Task 1 on the tape. Gesture for students to write the numbers.

6. (Optional) To make sure students understand what to do, stop after the second item. Ask students: *What's the number for the U.S. Consulate in São Paulo?* (Answer: 11-881-6511) Then play the rest of Listening Task 1.

7. If necessary, play Listening Task 1 a second time.

8. Check by having students call out the numbers. Write them on the board. (Answers appear in blue on the opposite page.)

ADDITIONAL SUPPORT Write the following dialog on the board:

A: Directory Assistance. May I help you?
B: Yes, I'd like the number for (A's name).
A: Just a moment, please. That's (A's phone number).
B: (Repeat A's number to check)?
A: That's right.

Have students stand and move around the room. They use the dialog to collect the numbers of at least ten other students. They write the numbers.

NOTES
- In North American English, the hyphen (–) in phone numbers isn't read. Rather, people pause between the area code and between the third and fourth digits.
- In telephone numbers, "zero" is usually pronounced "oh."

Culture corner

1. After students have read the Culture Corner, have them answer the questions in pairs or small groups: *Does your culture use 100 in this way? What are special numbers in your culture?* (Numbers can be "special" for any reason: Lucky and unlucky numbers are often the first things students think of.)

2. (Optional) Before class, make copies of the following paragraph. You'll need one copy for every two students.

Culture corner. Find the mistakes.

In the United States and Canada, 1000 is used to mean "often" or "many." Four example, a parent in the United States and Canada might say to a child, "I've told you 100 times not two do that!" Does you're culture use 100 in this way? What are special numbers in your culture?

In class, before they read the Culture Corner, give one copy to each pair. Tell them there are mistakes. They should try to find and correct the mistakes. Then they read the Culture Corner in the book to see if they were right.

Mistakes
1000 ⟶ 100
four ⟶ for
two ⟶ t wo
you're ⟶ your

LISTENING TASK 1

Information

❏ Listen. People want to know the telephone numbers for places in these cities. Write the telephone numbers.

1. Sydney, Australia
(02) 266 0610

2. São Paulo, Brazil
(11) 881-6511

3. Tokyo, Japan
3436-0901

4. Toronto, Canada
(416) 321-1234

5. Kuala Lumpur, Malaysia
293-5188

6. Mexico City, Mexico
203-9444

CULTURE CORNER

In the United States and Canada, "100" is used to mean "often" or "many." For example, a parent in the United States and Canada might say to a child, "I've told you 100 times not to do that!" Does your culture use 100 in this way? What are special numbers in your culture?

13

LISTENING TASK 2

The champions!

❏ Listen. These teams are in a basketball tournament. Write the scores.
Which team wins each game? Write the first letter of the team's name in the circle.

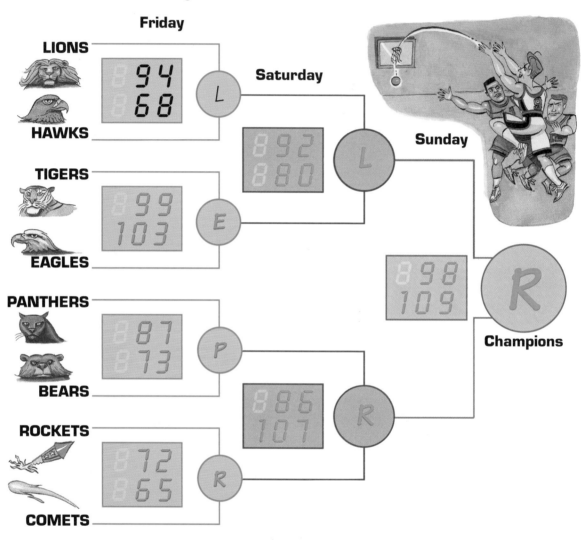

Friday

LIONS
94
68
HAWKS

L

Saturday

92
80

L

Sunday

TIGERS
99
103
EAGLES

E

98
109

R

Champions

PANTHERS
87
73
BEARS

P

86
107

R

ROCKETS
72
65
COMETS

R

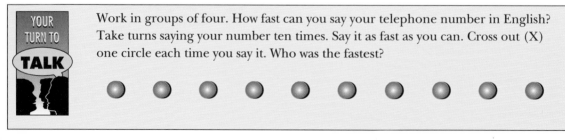

YOUR TURN TO TALK

Work in groups of four. How fast can you say your telephone number in English? Take turns saying your number ten times. Say it as fast as you can. Cross out (X) one circle each time you say it. Who was the fastest?

● ● ● ● ● ● ● ● ● ●

Listening Task 2
The champions!

Listening skill: Understanding sports scores

1. T: *Look at page 14.*

2. (Optional) Read the title: *"The champions!" What do you think this will be about?* Elicit answers from the students. (Answer: a sports [basketball] tournament/sports scores)

3. (Optional) If your students find listening very challenging, do the Additional Support procedure below.

4. Read the instructions: *Listen. These teams are in a basketball tournament. Write the scores. Which team wins each game? Write the first letter of the team's name in the circle.*

5. Play Listening Task 2 on the tape. Gesture for students to write the scores and to write the letters in the circles.

6. (Optional) To make sure students understand what to do, stop after the second game (Tigers vs. Eagles). Ask students: *What was the score?* (Answer: Tigers 99, Eagles 103) *The Eagles won, so write "E" in the circle.* Then play the rest of Listening Task 2.

7. If necessary, play Listening Task 2 a second time. Before replaying the tape, you may want to have students compare their answers in pairs: *Work with a partner. Look at your partner's answers. How many were the same? Then we'll listen again.*

8. Check by eliciting the scores and winners. Write them on the board in a pattern similar to the answers in the book. (Answers appear in blue on the opposite page.)

ADDITIONAL SUPPORT Have students look at the names of the teams. Tell them to listen to the tape once and raise their hands when they hear the team names.

Your turn to talk

1. Divide the class into groups of four. T: *How fast can you say your telephone number in English? Take turns saying your number ten times. Say it as fast as you can. Cross out one circle each time you say it. Who was the fastest?*

2. Demonstrate by drawing circles on the board and then saying your own number very quickly as you cross them out.

3. Have students do the activity.

Optional activity

(For use anytime during or after the unit.)

• **Fast math.** Before class, make copies of the "Fast Math Worksheet." You'll need one sheet for every three students. Students work in groups of three. One student is the quizmaster. Give that student the worksheet. The quizmaster gives the answer, then reads the two problems. The other partners race to see who can find the correct problem the fastest.

Fast Math Worksheet

You are the quizmaster. Read the answers. Then read both problems. Your partners will race to find which problem is correct.

Math words: + (plus)
$\quad$ - (minus)
$\quad$ **x** (times)

Answers	Problems		
a. 25	16 + 7	or	11 + 14*
b. 89	34 + 45	or	62 + 27*
c. 107	63 + 44*	or	46 + 51
d. 317	444 - 127	or	318 - 63*
e. 121	193 - 82	or	187 - 66*
f. 128	11 x 13	or	8 x 16*
g. s104	77 + 82	or	238 - 134*

* = Correct problems

© Cambridge University Press

UNIT 4
Let's eat!

Topic/function: Talking about food and places to eat

Listening skills: Inferring topics (Listening Task 1); understanding suggestions (Listening Task 2)

Grammar/vocabulary: *Let's . . .*, names of foods

Warming Up

1. Hold your book so that students can see page 15. T: *Look at page 15.*

2. Read the instructions. Pause when you see this symbol ♦ to give the students time to write their answers:

> *Work with a partner.*
> *These are some of the major food groups.*
> *Write the names in the boxes.* ♦
> *Do you know the names of the foods?*
> *Write them below.*
> *You can use your dictionary only two*
>   *times.* ♦

3. As students work, circulate and help pairs having difficulty. If there are foods they don't know how to say in English, encourage them to skip those items. Once they've identified the words they know, they can decide which two they want to look up in their dictionaries.

4. (Optional) T: *What other foods do you know that go in each group? Write as many as you can.*

5. Check by eliciting answers. (Answers appear in blue on the opposite page.)

Strategy exercise: *Listening for explanations and definitions*

Listening Task 1 presents foods that students may or may not know. Point out that a listener has to be patient sometimes and wait for the speaker to give a definition of an uncommon term. Speakers do not, of course, always do this

and, if they do not, it is the responsibility of the listener to ask for clarification. To get this point across, put students in pairs and have them select a common item. They should make up a new name (a nonsense word) for the item and write a set of clues for it. For example, they may re-name a pencil a "quom." They would then write clues like "A quom is useful when you have to take a test." or "A new quom is about 14 centimeters (5-1/2 inches) long." After they have written the clues, they work with another pair and see if that pair can guess their item from the context clues.

Optional activity

(For use anytime during or after the unit.)

• *Not a match game.* Make copies of the following worksheet. You'll need one for each student. Each student should first work individually to answer the questions on the worksheet. Then students work in groups of four or five to compare answers. Each student who has an answer that is different from all the others gets a point. The student with the most points in each group wins.

Not a Match Game Worksheet

Name . . .

1. a vegetable that is not green.
2. a food that tastes good on a hot day.
3. a food you do not like.
4. a food you would like to try (something you have never eaten).
5. a food that tastes good on a cold day.
6. something you eat in a restaurant, but never at home.
7. a food that smells good.
8. a food that smells bad.
9. a food that has a short season (you can eat it for only a short time each year).
10. a food that you eat for holidays.

© Cambridge University Press

Let's eat!

❏ Work with a partner.
These are some of the major food groups.
Write the names in the boxes.

vegetables   fruit   bread and grains
~~meat and fish~~   dairy

❏ Do you know the names of the foods?
Write them below.
You can use your dictionary only two times.

FOOD GROUPS

meat and fish

bread and grains

dairy

fruit

vegetables

① steak   ⑥ rolls   ⑪ apple
② chicken   ⑦ cheese   ⑫ banana
③ fish   ⑧ yogurt   ⑬ lettuce
④ bread   ⑨ milk   ⑭ carrots
⑤ rice   ⑩ orange   ⑮ peppers

LISTENING TASK 1

This tastes great!

Inferring topics

❏ Listen. People are eating different foods. They don't say the
names of the foods.
What are they talking about?
Number the pictures (1–6). There are two extra pictures.

2 pizza   6 fish   4 sushi (Japanese)

 hamburger   1 ice cream cone   soup

3 coffee   5 nan (Indian)

What foods are popular with young people in your country? What foods don't
most people like? These are the most and least popular foods for teenagers in
the United States and Canada.

CULTURE CORNER

Most popular
1. Italian food   5. seafood
2. steak   6. vegetables
3. hamburgers   7. potatoes
4. chicken/turkey   8. Mexican food

Least popular
1. spinach
2. liver
3. broccoli
4. vegetables in general

Do any of the answers surprise you? Which foods do you like and dislike?

16

Listening Task 1
This tastes great!

Note: The tapescript for Unit 4 begins on page T6.

1. T: *Look at page 16.*

2. (Optional) Read the title: *"This tastes great!" What do you think this will be about?* Elicit answers from the students. (Answers: foods people like, foods people are eating)

3. Read the instructions: *Listen. People are eating different foods. They don't say the names of the foods. What are they talking about? Number the pictures (1–6). There are two extra pictures.*

4. Play Listening Task 1 on the tape. Gesture for students to write the numbers in the boxes.

5. (Optional) To make sure students understand, stop after the first item (ice cream cone). T: *They never said "ice cream cone." What were the hints? How did you know they were talking about an ice cream cone?* Elicit answers (chocolate, vanilla, hot day).

6. (Optional) If your students find listening very challenging, do the Additional Support procedure below.

7. If necessary, play Listening Task 1 a second time. Before replaying the tape, you may want to have students compare their answers in pairs: *Work with a partner. Look at your partner's answers. How many were the same? How did your partner know? What were the hints? Then we'll listen again.*

8. Check by eliciting answers. Ask what the hints were (see Step 5). (Answers appear in blue on the opposite page.)

ADDITIONAL SUPPORT After showing how students can use inference (listening "between the lines") hints in Step 5, have students work in pairs. They look at the

pictures and write one or two words they might use for talking about each. Words might be food types (chocolate, vanilla), ingredients (on, for example, the pizza or hamburger), or things that are eaten with the food (cream and sugar with coffee).

NOTE

• Don't worry if some of the foods are unfamiliar to some students at the beginning of the lesson. Encourage students to see how much they can find out about the foods as they listen.

Culture corner

1. After students have read the Culture Corner, have them answer the questions in pairs or small groups: *Do any of the answers surprise you? Which foods do you like and dislike?*

2. (Optional) Make a few enlarged photocopies of Culture Corner. Post them on the front and back walls of the room. Tell students that the copies are a list of the most and least popular foods for U.S. and Canadian teenagers. Students work in pairs. One goes to the copy and reads the list, trying to remember as many of the foods as possible. That student goes back and dictates the foods to the partner who writes them. Then the second student goes to a copy, reads and tries to remember. That student returns and dictates. Students should work as quickly as possible. They continue until they've listed all twelve foods. When they finish, they check their books for accuracy of information and spelling.

Optional activity

(For use anytime during or after the unit.)

• ***What foods do you like?*** After reading Culture Corner, students work in small groups to rank the foods for themselves. They should agree on the top five first, then cut their list to the top three. They can also agree on their least favorite foods.

Listening Task 2
How about a pizza?

Listening skill: Understanding suggestions

1. T: *Look at page 17.*

2. (Optional) Read the title: *"How about a pizza?" What do you think this will be about?* Elicit answers from the students. (Answer: deciding on a restaurant)

3. (Optional) If your students find listening very challenging, do the Additional Support procedure below.

4. Read the instructions: *Listen. Some friends are deciding where to go to dinner. Cross out the places where they don't want to eat. Circle the place they choose. There is one extra place.*

5. Play Listening Task 2 on the tape. Gesture for students to cross out the places.

6. (Optional) To make sure students understand what to do, stop after the first item. T: *Which restaurant were they talking about? Will they go there? Why not?* Elicit answers (Mexican, no, not very good).

7. If necessary, play Listening Task 2 a second time. Before replaying the tape, you may want to have students compare their answers in pairs: *Work with a partner. Look at your partner's answers. How many were the same? Then we'll listen again.*

8. Check by eliciting answers. (Answers appear in blue on the opposite page.)

ADDITIONAL SUPPORT Have students close their books. They should listen one time. They raise their hands anytime they hear a word connected to food. It can be a food type (Mexican), a specific food (pizza), or a description (spicy). Having them raise their hands helps other students notice the key words.

Your turn to talk

1. Divide the class into pairs. T: *Work with a partner. Imagine that you and your partner are going on a picnic. You need to bring something that starts with every letter of the alphabet (except X). Take turns. How fast can you get to Z?*

2. (Optional) Demonstrate the first few letters of the alphabet with a student.

3. As students do the activity, circulate and give hints for letters students find challenging.

NOTES

• You may want to have students stand, face each other, and slap hands each time they say a sentence. The reason for slapping hands is that it adds a physical element that can make the activity more interesting. It also lets you know that everyone is doing the task and when they finish.

• Possible answers: apples, bananas, cake, doughnuts, eggs, fish, grapes, ham, ice cream, jelly, kiwi (or Kentucky Fried Chicken), lemons, milk, nuts, oranges, pumpkin, quiche, raisins, strawberries, turkey, udon noodles, vegetables, watermelon, yogurt, zucchini.

• The instructions don't actually say they can only bring food. If students choose something else for the more difficult letters, that's fine.

LISTENING TASK 2

How about a pizza?

❏ Listen. Some friends are deciding where to go to dinner.
Cross out (X) the places where they don't want to eat.
Circle the place they choose. There is one extra place.

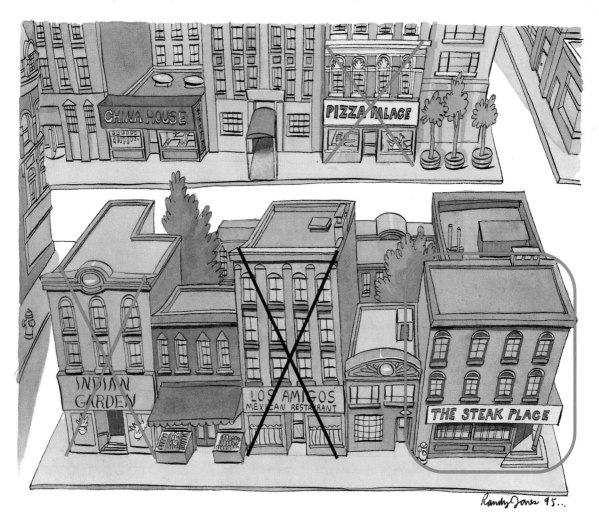

Randy Jones 95...

YOUR TURN TO TALK

Work with a partner. Imagine that you and your partner are going on a picnic. You
need to bring something that starts with every letter of the alphabet (except X).
Take turns. How fast can you get to Z?

Example
A: You bring the apples. I'll bring the bananas.
B: You bring the bananas. I'll bring the cake. . . .

Your free time

WARMING
UP

These words tell how often people do things.

always   sometimes   never

100%   0%

often   hardly ever

❏ Work with a partner.
How often do you do these things?
How often does your partner do them?
Draw lines.

	you	**your partner**
How often do you . . .	always never	always never
1. read magazines after dinner?		
2. play a sport on weekends?		
3. study English at night?		
4. watch TV on Saturday night?		
5. go to a restaurant for lunch?		
6. listen to music in the evening?		

Your free time

Topic/function: Talking about free-time
activities
Listening skills: Identifying frequency
(Listening Task 1); confirming and
revising predictions (Listening Task 2)
Grammar/vocabulary: Frequency adjectives

Warming Up

1. Hold your book so the students can see
page 18. T: *Look at page 18.*

2. Read the instructions. Pause when you
see the symbol ♦ to give students time to
answer the questions.

Work with a partner.
How often do you do these things?
How often does your partner do them?
Draw lines. ♦

3. (Optional) Demonstrate the first two
items with one student while the others
watch: *I usually read magazines after dinner.*
(Hold your book so they can see it and
draw a line). T: *How about you?*

4. As students work, circulate and help
pairs having difficulty.

5. It isn't really necessary to check this
activity since answers will vary. You might
want to do a general show of hands to see
which items are the most common.

NOTES

• This unit focuses on frequency. The
most common frequency adverbs are
"always," "usually," "often," "sometimes,"
"hardly ever," "never." Others include
"seldom," "rarely," "occasionally."

• Specific time periods are also used to
talk about frequency: "once a week,"
"every day," "a couple times a month."

Strategy exercise: Listening for a purpose

Each time they listen, students need to
know why they are listening. You can use
hypothetical situations to help students
learn this skill. Students can work in pairs
to answer the question, "In your own
language, what do you listen to each day?"
Some answers might be "I listen to the
weather report on the radio in the
morning," "I listen to the teacher tell us
about the homework," "I listen to my
friend tell me what she did last night."
After students list the ways they listen, have
them write down the information they
listen for (e.g., in the weather report, the
temperature or whether it's going to rain).

Optional activity

(For use anytime during or after the unit.)

• ***How many words?*** Write *Always* on one
side of the chalkboard and *Never* on the
other. Students work in pairs. On a piece
of paper, they write as many "words that
tell how often" (frequency adverbs) as
possible. They should write each word in
an appropriate position to show the
relationships. For example, "sometimes"
goes in the middle of the page and "often"
goes near "always." After they've written all
they can, students call out the words and
tell you where on the board to write them.
(See the Note above for a list of frequency
adverbs.)

Listening Task 1
How often?

Listening skill: Identifying frequency

Note: The tapescript for Unit 5 begins on page T8.

1. T: *Look at page 19.*

2. (Optional) Read the title: *"How often?" What do you think this will be about?* Elicit answers from the students. (Answer: how often people do various things)

3. (Optional) If your students find listening very challenging, do the Additional Support procedure below.

4. Read the instructions: *Listen. These people are talking about their free-time activities. How often do they do these things? Draw lines to show how often.*

5. Play Listening Task 1 on the tape. Gesture for students to draw lines.

6. (Optional) To make sure students understand what to do, stop after the second item. Have students compare with a partner to see if they drew lines in nearly the same place. Then play the rest of Listening Task 1.

7. If necessary, play Listening Task 1 a second time.

8. Check by writing *always* and *never* on the board. Leave some space between the words. Write *1* above *always* and *5* above *never*. Write *2*, *3*, and *4* between them. Have students call out the numbers to show where they drew their lines. (Answers appear in blue on the opposite page.)

ADDITIONAL SUPPORT As a full class, brainstorm frequency words (see Notes on the Warming Up lesson plan page). Write them on the board. Have students close their books. Play the tape once. Have them notice any frequency words they hear.

Culture Corner

1. After students have read the Culture Corner, have them answer the questions in pairs or small groups: *What kind of clubs do people in your country join? Are you a member of any clubs?*

2. (Optional) The examples here are very unusual clubs. After students have read the Culture Corner, have them work in pairs. Each pair should think of three strange or silly clubs. They write the clubs and rank them (1–3), with 1 being the most unusual. Each pair joins another pair. They combine lists and rank the clubs 1–6.

Optional activity

(For use anytime during or after the unit.)

• **Chalkboard race.** Students work in as many teams as there is space for at the chalkboard. One representative from each team will be writing at a time. Teams line up. Read one of the sentences below. The first person in line from each team runs to the chalkboard and answers the question truthfully. The first person to write a correct sentence wins a point for his or her team. Read the next sentence and the next member of each team answers.

How often do you . . .
1. watch sports on TV?
2. eat breakfast in a restaurant?
3. read a magazine in English?
4. listen to classical music?
5. watch news on TV?
6. walk to school?
7. exercise on the weekend?
8. cook dinner?

Continue with other questions from the unit or make up your own frequency questions.

LISTENING TASK 1

How often?

❑ Listen. These people are talking about their free-time activities.
How often do they do these things?
Draw lines to show how often.

1. read magazines after dinner

always   never

2. play a sport on weekends

3. study a language at night

4. watch TV on Saturday night

5. go to a restaurant for lunch

6. listen to music in the evening

CULTURE CORNER

Some people join clubs for their free-time activities. Clubs are groups of people with the same interests. There are many clubs for sports and music. In the United States and Canada, there are also some unusual clubs. There are even clubs for:

• people who have the same name
• people who love bananas
• people who hate mayonnaise
• adults who like to climb trees

What kind of clubs do people in your country join? Are you a member of any clubs?

I WANT TO JOIN!

LISTENING TASK 2

Which is more popular?

❏ People in the United States spend their free time in different ways.
Look at the questions. What do you think the answers will be?
Check (✔) your answers.

❏ Now listen. Circle the correct answers.
Write at least one extra fact about each item.

1. Which type of music do more people enjoy?
☐ Classical
☐ (Country and western)
☐ Rock
Fact: _59 % (like country)_

2. Why do most people listen to the radio?
☐ (For news)
☐ For entertainment
Fact: _92 % (listen for news)_

3. What type of magazines do more people read?
☐ (TV guides)
☐ News magazines
Fact: _17 million copies (sold each week)_

4. Which sport is more popular?
☐ (Swimming)
☐ Jogging
Fact: _17 % (like swimming)_

5. Which is true of more people?
☐ They never exercise in their free time.
☐ (They like to be active.)
Fact: _40 % (would rather be active)_

YOUR TURN TO TALK

Work in groups of about five. Think of a free-time activity. Find out who does it the most. Who does it the least? Stand in a line. The person who does the activity most is first. The person who does it least is last.

Example
A: How often do you listen to the radio?   C: How about you?
B: Every day.   D: Three times a week.

Listening Task 2
Which is more popular?

Listening skill: Confirming and revising
  predictions

1. T: *Look at page 20.*

2. (Optional) Read the title: *"Which is more popular?" What do you think this will be about?* Elicit answers from the students. (Answer: popularity of various free-time activities in the United States)

3. Read the instructions for Step One: *People in the United States spend their free time in different ways. Look at the questions. What do you think the answers will be? Check your answers.* **Note:** You may want students to do this step in pairs.

4. T: *Now listen. Circle the correct answers. Write at least one extra fact about each item.* Play Listening Task 2 on the tape. Gesture for students to circle the correct answers and to write extra information.

5. (Optional) If your students find listening very challenging, do the Additional Support procedure.

6. (Optional) Stop after the second item and ask a few students to read the extra fact they wrote.

7. (Optional) You may wish to stop the tape before each item and have a show of hands to see how many people guessed each answer.

8. If necessary, play Listening Task 2 a second time. Before replaying the tape, you may want to have students compare their answers in pairs: *Work with a partner. Look at your partner's answers. How many were the same? Then we'll listen again.*

9. Check by eliciting answers from the students. (Answers appear in blue on the opposite page.)

ADDITIONAL SUPPORT Have students do the entire activity in pairs. Each pair uses only one book. After each segment, pause the tape to give them time to think about what they heard and share the information with a partner. By letting their partners know what they hear, it becomes possible for students to compare their partners' information with that which they understood themselves.

NOTES

• Students should understand that this is a game, not a test. There is no reason they should know the information. Having them predict prepares them for the listening, gets them used to prediction as a strategy, and increases their interest.

• TV guides are magazines that list which shows are going to be on television during the week. They also contain stories about TV stars and shows. Some are sold in stores or by subscription. Others come as sections of newspapers.

• This information is about people living in the United States. It is based on data in *What Counts: The Complete Harper's Index* by C. Conn and H. Silverman (Holt) and *100% American* by E. Weiss (Poseidon Press).

• You may prefer to check after each item rather than waiting until students have heard all five parts.

Your turn to talk

1. Divide the class into groups of about five. T: *Think of a free-time activity. Find out who does it the most. Who does it the least? Stand in a line. The person who does the activity most is first. The person who does it least is last.*

2. (Optional) Demonstrate the activity by asking members of one group about a particular activity (e.g., studying English). Have them line up according to frequency.

3. (Optional) Have the students form lines for several different activities.

U N I T 6

That's a nice shirt.

Topic/function: Giving opinions about and describing clothing
Listening skills: Understanding descriptions of clothing (Listening Task 1); understanding reasons (Listening Task 2)
Grammar/vocabulary: Descriptive adjectives, clothing words

Warming Up

1. Hold your book so that students can see page 21. T: *Look at page 21.*

2. Read the instructions. Pause when you see the symbol ♦ to allow to give students time to write:

> *Work with a partner.*
> *Do you know the words for these clothes?*
> *Write as many as you can in three*
> *   minutes.* ♦

3. As students work, circulate and help pairs having difficulty. If there are words they don't know in English, encourage them to skip those items and go on to those they do know.

4. After three minutes, read the next part of the instructions:

> *Do you know these designs?*
> *Write the words.* ♦
> *Now change partners.*
> *Read your words. Listen to your partner's*
> *   words. Write any new words.*

5. Check by calling out the numbers and having students give their answers.

NOTES

• Many of the clothing items have more than one possible name. For example, for the first picture, the man's pants can also be called "slacks" or "trousers." Since the purpose of Warming Up is to activate vocabulary, encourage different answers.

• Some students may identify the third design as checked. Actually, it is plaid. The difference is that checked patterns usually have squares that are the same size. Plaid has overlapping squares of different sizes. Plaids often have several colors.

Strategy exercise: *Visualizing*

Having students visualize themselves doing an action or visualize themselves in a certain situation can help them remember related vocabulary. Brainstorm some clothing vocabulary on the board. Have everyone stand. First, together visualize a set ensemble (something unusual like blue and red striped pants and a checked green shirt). Visualize putting each piece of clothing on. Then students can try it for themselves with words they want to remember.

Optional activity

(For use anytime during or after the unit.)
• *Unusual clothes.* Write the following list of questions on the board:

> Why would you wear . . .
> >   a tuxedo to a basketball game?
> >   a bathing suit to the theater?
> >   a sweatsuit to a wedding?
> >   a long coat in summer?
> >   a sweater to the beach?

Ask students, in groups of three, to brainstorm reasons people might wear these clothes to these places. (Example: Someone might wear a tuxedo to a basketball game if he were going to sing the national anthem.) After the groups finish, they should work with others. Each group that came up with a reason the others did not gets a point. The group with the most points wins. One way to regroup is to number off within each group (You're number one, number two, number three). All the ones work together, all the twos, all the threes, etc.

That's a nice shirt.

❑ Work with a partner.
Do you know the words for these clothes?
Write as many as you can in three minutes.

① *jacket*
② *shirt*
③ *tie*
④ *pants*

⑤ *blouse*
⑥ *skirt*
⑦ *bag*
⑧ *shoes*

⑨ *cap*
⑩ *T-shirt*
⑪ *jeans*
⑫ *sneakers*

❑ Do you know these designs?
Write the words.

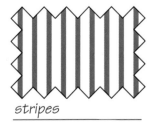

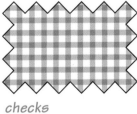

stripes

checks

plaid

❑ Now change partners.
Read your words. Listen to your partner's
words. Write any new words.

21

What are they wearing?

❑ Listen. What are Anna and Mike wearing today?
Circle your answers.

Anna

Mike

CULTURE CORNER

Even though people in both the United States and the United Kingdom speak English, they often use different words. Here are some words they use to talk about clothing:

U.S.	U.K.	U.S.	U.K.
cuffs (of pants)	turn-ups	bathing suit	swimming costume
stockings	tights	vest	waistcoat
pants	trousers	sneakers	plimsolls, pumps
suspenders	braces		

Are there any English words for clothing in your language? What are they?

Listening Task 1
What are they wearing?

Listening skill: Understanding descriptions of clothing

Note: The tapescript for Unit 6 begins on page T9.

1. T: *Look at page 22.*

2. (Optional) Read the title: *"What are they wearing?" What do you think this will be about?* Elicit answers from the students. (Answer: the clothes these people are wearing today)

3. (Optional) If your students find listening very challenging, do the Additional Support procedure below.

4. Read the instructions: *Listen. What are Anna and Mike wearing today? Circle your answers.*

5. Play Listening Task 1 on the tape. Gesture for students to circle their answers.

6. (Optional) To make sure students understand what to do, stop after the first two items. Ask students: *What is Anna wearing?* (Answers: white pants, a striped blouse) Then play the rest of Listening Task 1.

7. If necessary, play Listening Task 1 a second time.

8. Check by having students call out their answers. (Answers appear in black on the opposite page.)

ADDITIONAL SUPPORT Have students work in pairs. They look at the pictures and write two or three words about each item. What they write should include the name of the item and something (an adjective) that gives more information. For example, the bag could be a sports (or gym) bag, a large bag, or a green and purple bag. OR Have students close their books. Play the tape once. Students should raise their hands every time they hear an item of clothing mentioned.

NOTE

• You may wish to stop after the first section to check students' answers about Anna before going on to the information about Mike.

Culture corner

1. After students have read the Culture Corner, have them answer the questions in pairs or small groups: *Are there any English words for clothing in your language? What are they?*

2. (Optional) After students have read the Culture Corner, have them look at the map on pages 68–69. Remind them that English words have come from many languages and countries. Dictate the following words. Have them write each word on the place on the map they think it comes from.

Dictation words: cap, jacket, hat, jeans, jumper, pajamas, parka, shirt, skirt

Answers: cap – Italy (Latin)
jacket – France
hat – Iceland
jeans – Italy
jumper – Middle East (Arabic)
pajamas – India (Hindu)
parka – Canada/Alaska
           (Aleut [Eskimo])
shirt – Germany
skirt – Scandinavia
           (Norway/Sweden/Denmark)

Variation: An alternate way of doing the activity is to make copies of the dictation words and answers. Students work in groups of about four. One student reads the words. The others try to be the first to guess correctly. **Note:** This activity was developed by Mario Rinvolucri.

Listening Task 2
Dressing for work

Listening skill: Understanding reasons

1. T: *Look at page 23.*

2. (Optional) Read the title: *"Dressing for work." What do you think this will be about?* Elicit answers from the students. (Answer: casual clothes at work) Students may find it surprising that Dan is wearing casual clothes in his office. Have them guess why. (Answer: Casual clothes can be better for the environment.)

3. (Optional) If your students find listening very challenging, do the Additional Support procedure below.

4. Read the instructions: *Listen. On Fridays, people in Dan's office wear casual clothes to work. Dan is explaining why. Check his reasons.*

5. Play Listening Task 2 on the tape. Gesture for students to check their answers.

6. (Optional) To make sure students understand what to do, stop after the first item. Elicit students' answers. (Answer: Dry cleaning isn't necessary.) Then play the rest of Listening Task 2.

7. If necessary, play Listening Task 2 a second time.

8. Check by having students call out their answers. (Answers appear in blue on the opposite page.)

ADDITIONAL SUPPORT Have students work in groups of three. Students look at the pictures for one minute. Then they close their books and try to remember as much as possible. They should try to say what people are doing and wearing in as many pictures as possible.

NOTES

• Wearing casual clothes to work is increasingly popular in the United States.

In California, where many American trends begin, only 22% of men say they wear ties to work almost every day, 66% say they hardly ever do, and 11% say they wear ties a few days a week.

Your turn to talk

1. Divide the class into groups of three. T: *Work in groups of three. Look at everyone in the class for one minute. Try to remember what each person is wearing.*

2. (after one minute) T: *Now, two people in your group close their eyes. The other will person describe what someone is wearing. Try to guess who it is. Take turns.*

3. (Optional) Demonstrate by having everyone close their eyes. Describe someone and have students guess.

Optional activity

(For use anytime during or after the unit.)

• *A striped T-shirt and flowered pants?* In class, brainstorm words for clothing designs. Then, distribute enlarged copies of the picture below. Divide the class into pairs, Student A and Student B. A's draw the clothing designs for the boy's shirt, pants, and shoes. B's draw the designs for the girl's shirt, shorts, socks, and shoes. Each piece of clothing must be a different design. Then, in pairs, they describe the designs. Partners ask yes-no questions (Does he have a flowered shirt?) When the answer is yes, they draw the pattern.

Dressing for work

❏ Listen. On Fridays, people in Dan's office wear casual clothes to work. Dan is explaining why. Check (✔) his reasons.

1. With casual clothes . . .

☐ People seem friendlier.   ✔ Dry cleaning isn't necessary.   ☐ People save money.

2. At the office . . .

☐ People are more relaxed.   ☐ People can work harder.   ✔ Less air conditioning is necessary.

3. Getting to work . . .

✔ People can ride bicycles.   ☐ The trip takes less time.   ☐ The clothes are more comfortable for driving.

YOUR TURN TO TALK

Work in groups of three. Look at everyone in the class for one minute. Try to remember what each person is wearing. Now two people close your eyes. The other person will describe what someone is wearing. Try to guess who it is. Take turns.

Example
A: She's wearing a blue sweater.
B: Is it Naomi?

A: No. She's got white shoes on.
C: Is it Maria?
A: Yes, it is.

23

Furniture and houses

❑ Work with a partner.
These are four rooms in a house.
Write the names in the boxes.

~~bedroom~~   living room   kitchen   bathroom

❑ Do you know the names of the things in each room?
Write them below.

Rooms in a House

bedroom

bathroom

kitchen

living room

①	bed	⑤	toilet	⑨	floor
②	closet	⑥	refrigerator	⑩	sofa
③	dresser	⑦	sink	⑪	table
④	bathtub	⑧	stove	⑫	chair

24

Furniture and houses

Topic/function: Describing things in a house and what they are for
Listening skills: Inferring topics (Listening Task 1); understanding descriptions of things (Listening Task 2)
Grammar/vocabulary: Simple present for descriptions, names of furniture and rooms in a house

Warming Up

1. Hold your book so that students can see page 24. T: *Look at page 24.*

2. Read the instructions. Pause when you see the symbol ♦ so the students can write their answers:

Work with a partner.
These are four rooms in a house.
Write the names in the boxes.
bedroom, living room, kitchen, bathroom. ♦

3. Continue with the instructions:
Do you know the names of the things in each room?
Write them below. ♦

4. As students work, circulate and help pairs having difficulty.

5. (Optional) You may want to have students continue by listing additional pieces of furniture they would expect to find in each room.

6. Check by having a few students who finish early write the answers on the board.

NOTES

• Some of the objects have more than one name. For example, a "sofa" can also be called a "couch." Encourage various answers when possible.

• In daily use, "refrigerator" is often shortened to "fridge."

• Although "toilet" is the word for item #5, people in the United States rarely use the word. When asking the location, they usually say, "Where's the bathroom/ washroom/men's (or ladies') room?" etc.

Strategy exercise: *Taking a tour*
Another way to remember words through visualization is to "walk through" a place. Have students think of a piece of furniture. (Example: a desk) Tell them not to "go" directly to the desk, but instead "walk" in their mind's eye through the front door of their home through all the rooms, naming the objects they "see" in English, until they reach the desk.

Optional activity
(For use anytime during or after the unit.)
• **Furniture pantomime.** Before class, make copies of the worksheets below. Students work in pairs. They take turns pantomiming the objects on their list. Their partner may need to ask, "How do you say ___ in English?"

To help them get started, begin by pantomiming a coffee table. Have students guess.

Furniture pantomime
Worksheet A
Pantomime the following pieces of furniture. Your partner will guess.

1. a dining room table   5. a bed
2. a stereo/CD player   6. a microwave
3. a bathroom sink   oven
4. a desk

Worksheet B
Pantomime the following pieces of furniture. Your partner will guess.

1. a TV   5. a mirror
2. a lamp   6. a coffee
3. a kitchen table   maker
4. a bathtub

© Cambridge University Press

Listening Task 1
What are they talking about?

Listening skill: Inferring topics

Note: The tapescript for Unit 7 begins on page T10.

1. T: *Look at page 25.*

2. (Optional) Read the title: "*What are they talking about?*" *What do you think this will be about?* Elicit answers from the students. (Answer: furniture and other things in houses)

3. (Optional) If your students find listening very challenging, do the Additional Support procedure.

4. Read the instructions: *People are talking about furniture and other things in houses. What are they talking about? Number the pictures (1–5). There are four extra pictures.*

5. Play Listening Task 1 on the tape. Gesture for students to number the pictures.

6. (Optional) Since this is an inference (listening "between the lines") activity, it may be useful to stop after the first item to check that students understand. Elicit answers from the students. To help others who found it difficult, ask a few students who got the answer what clues on the tape helped them figure it out. (Possible answers: room in the top part; put things like glasses, cups, dishes in it; shelves, pots and pans)

7. If necessary, play Listening Task 1 a second time. Before replaying the tape, you may want to have students compare their answers in pairs: *Work with a partner. Look at your partner's answers. How many were the same? How did you know? What words gave you hints? Then we'll listen again.*

8. Check by having students call out their answers. Again, you may want to ask them which words gave them the hints. (Answers appear in blue on the opposite page.)

ADDITIONAL SUPPORT Write the following on the board:

You use it to _____.
It's usually made of _____.

Students work in groups of three. One person thinks of one of the items on this page or on page 24. That person gives hints by completing the sentences on the board. Partners race to guess. They take turns.

NOTE

• Make sure students understand that this is an inference activity. The names of the furniture and appliances are not said directly. For more ideas on introducing listening to infer, see the lesson plan pages 3 and 4 of this manual.

Culture corner

1. After students have read the Culture Corner, have them answer the question in pairs or small groups: *How big is an average house in your country?*

2. (Optional) After students have read the Culture Corner, tell them you are going to read it again. You will make some mistakes. They should listen and find your mistakes. Read the following ("mistakes" are underlined):

T: *How big is your house? In the United States and Canada, people usually say, "I have a three-bedroom <u>home</u>" or "I have a two-bedroom apartment." They count the number of <u>beds</u>. This tells you the size of their house. In <u>Korea</u>, people say, "I have a <u>2DLK</u>" or "I have a 1DK." DK means dining room/kitchen. LDK means living room/dining room/kitchen. The number tells you how many other rooms they have. For example, a 1DK is a small <u>house</u> with one room plus a dining room/kitchen. How big is an average house in your country?*

• As a follow-up to the above activity, have students change a few words in the paragraph and read it to each other, in pairs. Partners try to find the mistakes.

LISTENING TASK 1

What are they talking about?

❏ People are talking about furniture and other things in houses.
What are they talking about? Number the pictures (1–5).
There are four extra pictures.

 `2` a sofa

 ☐ a frying pan

 `4` a folding chair

 ☐ a bed

 ☐ an armchair

 `1` a cabinet

 `5` a lamp

 ☐ a heater

 `3` an air conditioner

 CULTURE CORNER

How big is your house? In the United States and Canada, people usually say, "I have a three-bedroom house" or "I have a two-bedroom apartment." They count the number of bedrooms. This tells you the size of their house. In Japan, people say, "I have a 2LDK" or "I have a 1DK." DK means dining room/kitchen. LDK means living room/dining room/kitchen. The number tells you how many other rooms they have. For example, a 1DK is a small apartment with one room plus a dining room/kitchen. How big is an average house in your country?

25

LISTENING TASK 2

Where's the heater?

Around the world, people keep their houses warm in different ways.

❑ Listen. Where are the heaters in these rooms?
Circle them. If there is no heater, check (✔) "none."

1. Syria

☐ none

2. Germany

☐ none

3. Korea

☐ none

4. Brazil

✔ none

5. Japan

☐ none

YOUR TURN TO TALK

Work in pairs. What's your favorite room in your house or apartment? What does it look like? Tell your partner about your favorite room. Your partner will listen and draw a picture of it. Take turns.

Example: My favorite room is the kitchen. I really like to cook. The kitchen is big. There are lots of windows. . . .

Listening Task 2
Where's the heater?

Listening skill: Understanding descriptions of things

1. T: *Look at page 26.*

2. (Optional) Read the title: *"Where's the heater?" What do you think this will be about?* Elicit answers from the students. (Answer: the location of heaters in houses in various countries)

3. (Optional) If your students find listening very challenging, do the Additional Support procedure below.

4. Read the instructions: *Around the world, people keep their houses warm in different ways. Listen. Where are the heaters in these rooms? Circle them. If there is no heater, check "none."*

5. Play Listening Task 2 on the tape. Gesture for students to circle the heaters.

6. (Optional) To make sure students understand what to do, stop after one or two items. Ask students: *Where is the heater?* When they answer, point to it in your book. Then play the rest of Listening Task 2.

7. If necessary, play Listening Task 2 a second time.

8. Check by having students call out their answers. Point to them in your book. (Answers appear in black on the opposite page.)

ADDITIONAL SUPPORT Have students work in pairs. They put one copy of the book, open to page 26, between them. They try to decide the location of the heater. As they talk, they must not touch the pictures. This is necessary so that they use the vocabulary (both the things in the picture and prepositions of location) that they will hear when they listen. It doesn't matter if they happen to predict correctly.

The act of predicting will get them more involved with the task and will often focus their listening and increase their interest.

NOTES

• Naturally, various types of heaters are used in these countries. Those included in this activity are examples of one type.

• You may prefer to check answers after each segment rather than waiting until students have heard all five parts.

Your turn to talk

1. Divide the class into pairs. T: *Work in pairs. What's your favorite room in your house or apartment? What does it look like? Tell your partner about your favorite room. Your partner will listen and draw a picture of it. Take turns.*

2. (Optional) Demonstrate by describing your favorite room. Students draw it.

NOTES

• Students who are good at drawing sometimes take too long with art-based activities since they want the picture to be "perfect." A way around this problem is to forbid the use of erasers. Once a line is drawn, it can't be changed.

Optional activities

(For use anytime during or after the unit.)

• *Fire!* Students work in groups. They tell their group about what they would save if a fire threatened their house.

• *A traditional house.* Students work in pairs. They talk about traditional houses in their countries. Each pair should make a list of things in a traditional house. They should list as many things as possible in five minutes. Then they join another pair and combine lists. Finally, students imagine they are building a new, modern house. They decide what traditional things they would want in it.

How do you start your day?

> **Topic/function:** Talking about routines
> **Listening skills:** Identifying routines (Listening Task 1); understanding questions about activities (Listening Task 2)
> **Grammar/vocabulary:** Simple present, sequence markers (*first, then, next,* etc.), simple past

Warming Up

1. Hold your book so that students can see page 27. T: *Look at page 27.*

2. Read the instructions. Pause when you see the symbol ♦ to give students time to answer the questions.

> *What do you do in the morning?*
> *What do you do first? After that? Number the actions. Cross out the things that you don't do.* ♦

3. After about one minute, continue with the instructions at the bottom of the page:

> *Work with a partner.*
> *Read your sentences in order (one, two, three, and so on).*
> *Add one of these words to each sentence: first, then, next, after that, finally.*

4. As students work, circulate and help pairs having difficulty.

5. It isn't necessary to check this activity. However, it may be of interest to have a show of hands to see how many people do each activity. OR See the Optional Activity "Most of us . . . ," at right.

NOTES

• Encourage pairs that finish Warming Up early to add additional activities that they usually do in the morning.

• A possible follow-up for this page is a "Find someone who" activity. Students stand and circulate. They ask the questions ("Do you make coffee in the morning?"). Partners must answer, adding extra information rather than just saying "yes" or "no." ("Yes, I drink two cups of coffee" or "No, I usually drink tea.") When someone says, "Yes" the partner writes his or her name and the extra information. They then change partners. Each name can only be used one time. (See the Unit 1 Your Turn to Talk on page 8 for a more complete explanation of "Find someone who.")

Strategy exercise: *Using the body as well as the mind*

One way to learn new words is to act them out. The motion is another clue to remembering the word. Divide students into an even number of small groups. Each group selects a series of daily routines. One group acts out the routine for another group while the second group tries to guess the words.

Optional activity

(For use anytime during or after the unit.)

• **Most of us . . . .** Write the following on the board: *All of us . . ., Most of us. . ., Some of us . . ., A few of us . . ., None of us . . . .* After students have done the Warming Up activity but before you've done Step 5 of the lesson plan, have them continue in pairs. They look at each item and guess how many other class members do the activity each morning. They write one of the phrases next to each item. When they have finished guessing, have them raise their hands for each activity they do. They check their guesses to see how often they were right.

How do you start your day?

❑ What do you do in the morning?
What do you do first? After that? Number the actions.
~~Cross out~~ the things that you don't do.

☐ I make coffee.   ☐ I exercise.   ☐ I watch TV.

☐ I read the newspaper.   ☐ I eat breakfast.

☐ I listen to the radio.   ☐ I take a shower.

❑ Work with a partner.
Read your sentences in order (1, 2, 3, etc.).
Add one of these words to each sentence:
first, then, next, after that, finally.

Example: First, I take a shower. Then I . . .

27

And after that?

❏ Listen to these people. In what order do they do things?
Write the numbers (1–3). There is one extra item for each.

1. What does Eric do in the morning?

- ☐ 2 He eats breakfast.
- ☐ 1 He takes a shower.
- ☐ He listens to the radio.
- ☐ 3 He reads the newspaper.

2. What does Anne do in the morning?

- ☐ She watches TV.
- ☐ 3 She goes to work.
- ☐ 1 She makes coffee.
- ☐ 2 She exercises.

3. What does Karen do after school?

- ☐ 2 She eats dinner.
- ☐ 3 She watches TV.
- ☐ She listens to music.
- ☐ 1 She studies.

4. What does Joel do in the evening?

- ☐ 1 He eats dinner.
- ☐ 3 He reads.
- ☐ He watches TV.
- ☐ 2 He puts his children to bed.

CULTURE CORNER

Here are some sayings about waking up early:
- "The early bird gets the worm."
- "Early to bed and early to rise makes one healthy, wealthy, and wise."

Do you agree with these sayings? Do you like to wake up early? Does your culture have any sayings like these?

Listening Task 1
And after that?

> **Listening skill:** Identifying routines

Note: The tapescript for Unit 8 begins on page T11.

1. T: *Look at page 28.*

2. (Optional) Read the title: *"And after that?" What do you think this will be about?* Elicit answers from the students. (Answer: people's daily routines)

3. (Optional) If your students find listening very challenging, do the Additional Support procedure below.

4. Read the instructions: *Listen to these people. In what order do they do things? Write the numbers, 1 through 3. There is one extra item for each.*

5. Play Listening Task 1 on the tape. Gesture for students to number the sentences.

6. (Optional) To make sure students understand what to do, stop after the first item. Ask students: *What does Eric do next?* (Answer: He eats breakfast.) *And after that?* (Answer: He reads the newspaper.) Then play the rest of Listening Task 1.

7. If necessary, play Listening Task 1 a second time.

8. Check by asking questions as in Step 6 and having students call out the answers. (Answers appear in blue on the opposite page.)

ADDITIONAL SUPPORT Individually, students read though the items for all four people. They write "Y" (for "yes") or "N" (for "no") next to each, depending on whether or not they themselves do the activity at the time indicated (morning, after school, evening).

Culture corner

1. After students have read the Culture Corner, have them answer the questions in pairs or small groups: *Do you agree with these sayings? Do you like to wake up early? Does your culture have any sayings like these?*

2. (Optional) Understanding the rhythm of English is a useful step for students. After they have read the Culture Corner, read it to them. Pause slightly when you see this mark: //. Students listen and mark the pauses. They then try reading Culture Corner aloud in pairs, pausing correctly.

T: *Here are some sayings // about waking up // early.// "The early bird // gets the worm."//"Early to bed // and early to rise // makes one healthy, // wealthy, // and wise." Do you agree // with these sayings? // Do you like // to wake up early? // Does your culture // have any sayings // like these?*

NOTES

• The first saying is also phrased as "The early bird catches the worm."

• The second saying is by Benjamin Franklin, an American writer, inventor, and statesman. Someone has created a parody of the proverb: "Early to rise and late to bed, makes one unhealthy, wealthy, and dead." You may wish to write the parody version on the board to use as the example for Step 2 of the Culture Corner plan.

Optional activity

(For use anytime during or after the unit.)

• *Everybody is a star.* Students work in small groups. Each student role-plays a different celebrity (of their own choosing). The members of the group interview each other about their daily routines.

Listening Task 2
And then I . . .

1. T: *Look at page 29.*

2. (Optional) Read the title: *"And then I . . ." What do you think this will be about?* Elicit answers from the students. (Answer: the students' own routine yesterday)

3. (Optional) If your students find listening very challenging, do the Additional Support procedure below.

4. Read the instructions: *Think about yesterday. What did you do? You are going to write about your day. Listen. Write your answers.*

5. Play Listening Task 2 on the tape. Gesture for students to write their answers. If necessary, pause the tape between items to give more time to write. Make sure students know that they can write short answers, not full sentences.

6. (Optional) To make sure students understand that this is a personalized activity, stop after the first item. Ask two or three students: *What time did you get up yesterday?* Then play the rest of Listening Task 2.

7. If necessary, play Listening Task 2 a second time.

8. Check by asking students what they wrote for each item. You may want to write the topics on the board. (Topics appear in blue on the opposite page.)

ADDITIONAL SUPPORT Write the following words on the board: *What . . .? Was . . .? Did . . .? Where . . .?*

Students close their books and copy the words. Play the entire Listening Task 2 segment. Students make a mark each time they hear one of the words.

Answers: What (7 [8 if the "What" in the instructions is included]), Was (2), Did (22 [23 if the "Did" in the instructions is included]), Where (1). OR As above, but students simply raise their hands each time they hear one of the words.

NOTE

• Step 5 of the lesson plan mentions pausing the tape to give more time for writing. Part of being a fluent listener is responding quickly. Giving too much time can allow students to try to analyze and/or translate every word, an unproductive listening habit.

Your turn to talk

1. Divide the class into groups of three. T: *Work in groups of three. Look at your answers to Listening Task 2. Tell your partners what you did yesterday. Use words like these:* first, then, next.

2. (after about five minutes) T: *Listen to your partners. How many things were the same?*

3. (Optional) Demonstrate by directing one group though Step 1 of the lesson plan as the others watch.

NOTE

• It doesn't matter if students go through their entire day in turns or if they alternate with each person mentioning the time they get up, what they ate for breakfast, etc. Whichever way they do the activity, they should react to what their partners are saying.

Optional activity

(For use anytime during or after the unit but particularly good as a follow-up to Your Turn to Talk.)

• *Tell a lie.* Students work in pairs. They tell their partner about their daily routine, but they should change three facts. The partner tries to guess the three "lies."

LISTENING TASK 2
And then I . . .

❏ Think about yesterday. What did you do?
You are going to write about your day.

❏ Listen. Write your answers.

1. *(time student woke up)* _____

2. *(things student ate for breakfast)* _____

3. *(two things student did in the*
morning) _____

4. *(one thing student did in the*
afternoon) _____

5. *(things student did last night)* _____

6. *(time student went to bed)* _____

YOUR TURN TO TALK

Work in groups of three. Look at your answers to Listening Task 2. Tell your partners what you did yesterday. Use words like these: *first, then, next.* Listen to your partners. How many things were the same?

Example
A: First, I . . .
B: I did that, too.

I'd like to see that!

❑ Work with a partner.
What kind of movie do you like best? Circle it.
What kind of movie does your partner like best? Draw
a star (★) next to it.

❑ Write one thing about each kind of movie.
For example: (science-fiction movies)
• something you usually see in that kind of movie (robots)
• the name of a movie (*Star Wars*)
• a famous movie star (Harrison Ford)

SAMPLE
ANSWERS

Science-fiction movies

robots

Love stories

Paris

Action movies

car chases

Musicals

dancing

Classics

a love story

Comedies

Charlie Chaplin

UNIT 9
I'd like to see that!

Topic/function: Giving opinions about movies
Listening skills: Understanding responses (Listening Task 1); inferring kinds of movies, understanding evaluations (Listening Task 2)
Grammar/vocabulary: Movie genres

Warming Up

1. Hold your book so that students can see page 30. T: *Look at page 30.*

2. Read the instructions. Pause when you see the symbol ♦ to give students time to answer the questions.

> *Work with a partner.*
> *What kind of movie do you like best? Circle it.*
> *What kind of movie does your partner like best?*
> *Draw a star next to it.* ♦

3. (after about one minute) Read the rest of the instructions:

> *Write one thing about each kind of movie.*
> *For example: science fiction movies.*
> *You could write something you usually see in that kind of movie (robots).*
> *You could write the name of a movie (Star Wars).*
> *You could write the name of a famous movie star (Harrison Ford)* ♦

4. (Optional) You may want to do the "Love stories" item as a full class brainstorm to give students ideas about different things they could write.

5. As students work, circulate and help pairs having difficulty.

6. Check as a group brainstorm. OR Have some pairs that finish early write their answers on the board as examples.

NOTES

• Of course, students can think about movies they've seen on TV or video as well as those seen in a theater. If they have difficulty thinking of movies, they can also use TV shows.

• The terms "movie" and "film" have about the same meaning in American English. Very artistic productions are often referred to as "films" rather than "movies." "Cinema" isn't usually used in American English to refer to films, but it is sometimes used in the names of movie theaters.

Strategy exercise: *Summarizing*

As homework, have students watch a video or TV program in English or listen to an English song or radio broadcast. Ask them to write a summary of what they heard and share it with their classmates in groups. They should prepare a list of words in the summary their classmates might not know.

Watching a TV program or video in English can be very challenging. One way to make it more understandable is for students to watch a video with subtitles in their own language, then cover the subtitles and watch it again. Another option, if students have bilingual televisions available, is to watch the news, first in their first language and then in English (or in the other order, first watching in English, then in their first language to confirm).

While the above ideas make use of the students' native languages, they also help with English since the summarizing task is done in English.

Optional activity

(For use anytime during or after the unit.)

• ***Starring Kevin Costner as you!*** Students work in small groups to decide which famous actors would play them in a movie. They then sketch out the story of the movie.

Listening Task 1
Let's go!

Listening skill: Understanding responses

Note: The tapescript for Unit 9 begins on page T12.

1. T: *Look at page 31.*

2. (Optional) Read the title: *"Let's go!" What do you think this will be about?* Elicit answers from the students. (Answer: inviting people to go to the movies)

3. (Optional) If your students find listening very challenging, do the Additional Support procedure below.

4. Read the instructions: *Listen. Some friends are talking about movies. Are they going to see the movies together? Check "yes" or "no."*

5. Play Listening Task 1 on the tape. Gesture for students to check their answers.

6. (Optional) To make sure students understand what to do, stop after the second item. Ask students: *Are they going to see the movie together?* (Answer: yes) Then play the rest of Listening Task 1.

7. If necessary, play Listening Task 1 a second time.

8. Check by having students call out their answers. (Answers appear in blue on the opposite page.)

ADDITIONAL SUPPORT Have students work in pairs. They look at the pictures and guess what type of film each is. Students can use the movie categories from page 30 or other terms they know. They may make mistakes. For example, they might think number 1 is an action film or a classic, rather than a comedy. However, even if their guesses are wrong, the task still gets them thinking about the film content.

NOTE

• Some teachers may object to the nature of certain films here (horror and action films). They are included in this lesson because they are popular with a great many people. Depending on your teaching situation and students' interests, this might serve as an opportunity to discuss whether or not they believe that violence in films and on TV is dangerous, leading to real violence.

Culture corner

1. After students have read the Culture Corner, have them answer the questions in pairs or small groups: *Have you seen any of these movies? What movies are "classics" in your country?*

2. (Optional) Before students have read the Culture Corner, write the names of the films on the board: *E.T., Star Wars, Jaws, The Sound of Music, Gone With the Wind, Snow White.* Students work in pairs. They write down anything they know about the films in five minutes. OR Write the dates on the board in chronological order: *1937, 1939, 1965, 1975, 1977, 1982.* Students try to match the dates and the movies. Then they read to check their guesses.

NOTE

• Some of these films may have been released under different titles in the students' countries. Make sure students know what films they are reading about

Optional activity

(For use anytime during or after the unit.)

• *The greatest movies of all time.* Students work in pairs to decide the five greatest movies they've ever seen, then regroup with another pair to make a list of three movies they agree on.

LISTENING TASK 1

Let's go!

❏ Listen. Some friends are talking about movies.
Are they going to see the movies together? Check (✔) "yes" or "no."

1. ☐ yes   ☑ no

2. ☑ yes   ☐ no

3. ☐ yes   ☑ no

4. ☑ yes   ☐ no

5. ☐ yes   ☑ no

6. ☐ yes   ☑ no

Some movies are classics. Even though they aren't new, millions of people around the world still enjoy watching them. Some people watch them in theaters. Others watch them on video. What are the most popular films of all time? These are the most popular in the United States and Canada:

- *E.T. The Extra-Terrestrial* (1982)
- *Star Wars* (1977)
- *Jaws* (1975)
- *The Sound of Music* (1965)
- *Gone With the Wind* (1939)
- *Snow White* (1937)

Have you seen any of these movies? What movies are "classics" in your country?

31

A night at the movies

Film critics watch movies.
They tell people if the films are good or bad.

❑ Listen. What kinds of movies are the film critics talking about?
Check (✔) them.

❑ Do the critics like the films?
Write "yes" or "no."

THE FILM CRITICS

	Jean	Robert
1. *Beyond the Stars* ☐ horror ✔ science fiction	*yes*	*yes*
2. *Another Fine Mess* ✔ comedy ☐ love story	*yes*	*no*
3. *My Guy* ✔ musical ☐ classic	*yes*	*yes*
4. *Crack Up* ✔ action ☐ comedy	*no*	*no*
5. *Just You and Me* ✔ love story ☐ musical	*no*	*no*

YOUR TURN TO TALK

Work with a partner. Tell your partner five things about your favorite movie. Use sentences like these:

My favorite movie is _____ .　　The movie is about _____ .
It stars *(names of actors)* .　　I like it because _____ .

Now work with another partner. Describe your first partner's favorite movie.

Listening Task 2
A night at the movies

> **Listening skills:** Inferring kinds of movies, understanding evaluations

1. T: *Look at page 32.*

2. (Optional) Read the title: *"A night at the movies." What do you think this will be about?* Elicit answers from the students. (Answer: movie reviews)

3. (Optional) If your students find listening very challenging, do the Additional Support procedure below.

4. Read the instructions: *Film critics watch movies. They tell people if the films are good or bad. Listen. What kinds of movies are the film critics talking about? Check them. Do the critics like the films? Write "yes" or "no."*

5. Play Listening Task 2 on the tape. Gesture for students to check the film types and write the critics opinions.

6. (Optional) To make sure students understand what to do, stop after the second item. Ask students: *What kind of movie is* Another Fine Mess*? Does Jean like* Another Fine Mess*? Does Robert?* (Answers: comedy, yes, no) Then play the rest of Listening Task 2.

7. If necessary, play Listening Task 2 a second time. Before replaying the tape, you may want to have students compare their answers in pairs: *Work with a partner. Look at your partner's answers. How many were the same? Then we'll listen again.*

8. Check by having students call out their answers. (Answers appear in blue on the opposite page.)

ADDITIONAL SUPPORT Have students do the activity as two separate tasks. The first time, they are only trying to find out the film type. They should do this in pairs, noting words that gave them the hints.

Then they listen again for the critics opinions. OR Have students look at the film types listed after each title. In pairs, they write one thing they would expect to hear about each type.

NOTES

• The first step of each item (identifying the film types) is inference (listening "between the lines"). It may be useful to have students notice the words that gave them the clues.

• The film titles in this listening task and Listening Task 1 are not real movies.

Your turn to talk

1. Divide the class into pairs. T: *Work with a partner. Tell your partner five things about your favorite movie.*

2. (Optional) Give an example by talking about a movie you like. Use sentences like these: *My favorite movie is _____. It stars _____. The movie is about _____. I like it because _____.*

3. (after about five minutes) T: *Now work with another partner. Describe your first partner's favorite movie.*

4. (Optional) Have students continue with several different partners.

NOTE

• If you decide to have students continue talking to different partners (Step 4, above), it may be useful to set a time limit (about one minute) for each interaction. If students are sitting in rows, have them stand and face their partners. At the end of the time limit, the students in one row move in the same direction to face the next partner. Because they are telling about the same film several times, most students are able to add extra information as the activity progresses because it gets easier each time they tell about the film.

UNIT 10
Where is it?

Topics/functions: Describing location and
  giving directions
Listening skills: Following directions
  (Listening Task 1); identifying locations
  (Listening Task 2)
Grammar/vocabulary: Imperatives,
  prepositions of location

Warming Up

1. Hold your book so that students can see
page 33. T: *Look at page 33.*

2. Read the instructions:

> *Look at these words: in, on, under, between,*
>   *next to. Do you know these prepositions?*
> *Look at the picture for one minute.*
> *There are many mistakes in it.*
> *Try to remember the mistakes.*

3. (after exactly one minute) Read the rest
of the instructions:

> *Now work with a partner.*
> *Close your book.*
> *What were the mistakes? Make sentences with*
>   *the prepositions and these words: calendar,*
>   *ceiling, chair, coffee table, dog, fishbowl,*
>   *floor, motorcycle, sofa, TV, TV stand, vase.*

4. As students work, copy the above words
on the board as a reminder. Then circulate
and help pairs having difficulty.

5. After pairs have remembered all the
mistakes, they can look back at their books
to check.

NOTES

• Most students will already know the
prepositions at the top of the page. If
there are any nouns at the bottom that
they might not know, pre-teach them.

• Listening Task 1 focuses on
prepositions of location and prepositional
phrases (past, next, across from, on the
left, etc.). Listening Task 2 also includes
imperatives (Cross the bridge, Continue

along the path, etc.). Note that the subject
of imperatives in English is "you" but is not
usually stated. When "you" is stated as the
subject of an imperative, it often sounds
angry: "You come here!"

Sample Answers

The dog is in the fishbowl.
The calendar is on the floor.
The chair is on the ceiling.
The motorcycle is next to the sofa.
The TV is under the TV stand.
The vase is between the sofa and the
  coffee table.

Strategy exercise: *Focusing on specific words*

This might be a good time to recycle the
idea of focusing on specific words. Students
should anticipate the information they
need. Tell them to listen to the tape once
with their eyes closed. Have them note how
many times they hear prepositions and
direction words. In Listening Task 2, they
can point right, left or straight ahead when
they hear those words to add a physical
component to the activity.

Optional activity

(For use anytime during or after the unit.)

• *It was there.* Begin by bringing in several
interesting objects. Put them on a table in
front of the class. Ask students to describe
the locations of the items. Then cover the
items with a sheet or towel and rearrange
them. Take off the cover. Students try to
remember where the items were. Students
then work in groups of about four. They
each contribute three items from their
pockets or bookbags. One person arranges
the items and gives the others a chance to
look at the arrangement. Then the items
are covered and rearranged. The members
of the group try to remember where things
were (The eraser is on the pencil. It was to
the right of the pencil.).

Where is it?

☐ Look at these words. Do you know these prepositions?

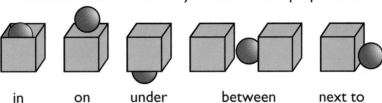

in   on   under   between   next to

☐ Look at the picture for one minute.
There are many mistakes in it.
Try to remember the mistakes.

☐ Now work with a partner.
Close your book.
What were the mistakes? Make sentences with the
prepositions and these words:

calendar	coffee table	floor	TV
ceiling	dog	motorcycle	TV stand
chair	fishbowl	sofa	vase

Example: The dog is in the fishbowl.

I'm lost!

❑ Listen. People are looking for places.
Where are the places? Check (✔) the correct circles.

1. The Four Seasons Restaurant

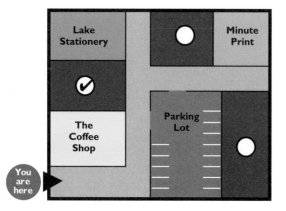

2. The Century Hotel

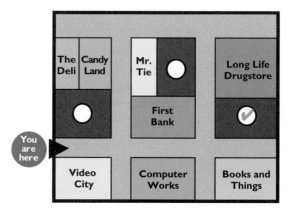

3. a drugstore

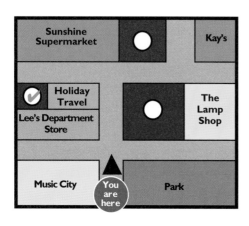

4. a video store

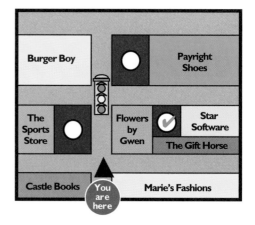

CULTURE CORNER

In some languages, people use polite words like "please" when giving directions. ("Please turn right at the corner.") In English, this sounds strange. "Please" is only used for things that help the speaker, not the listener. ("Please tell me how to get there.") Directions are usually given simply. ("Turn right at the corner.") How do you give directions in your language?

Listening Task 1
I'm lost!

Note: The tapescript for Unit 10 begins on page T14.

1. T: *Look at page 34.*

2. (Optional) Read the title: *"I'm lost!"* *What do you think this will be about?* Elicit answers from the students. (Answer: following directions)

3. (Optional) If your students find listening very challenging, do the Additional Support procedure below.

4. Read the instructions: *Listen. People are looking for places. Where are the places? Check the correct circles.*

5. Play Listening Task 1 on the tape. Gesture for students to check the circles.

6. (Optional) To make sure students understand what to do, stop after the second item and ask: *Where's the Century Hotel?* Elicit responses. (Answer: next to a drugstore, across the street from a bank) Then play the rest of Listening Task 1.

7. If necessary, play Listening Task 1 a second time.

8. Check by making a quick sketch of the maps on the board. Have students give answers. **Note:** Although it is quicker to have the students simply check the circles, they will get more language practice if you insist that they explain where things are. (Example: The restaurant is on the left, past the coffee shop.) (Answers appear in blue on the opposite page.)

ADDITIONAL SUPPORT As a full class, brainstorm phrases they would use to give directions (Go straight, Turn right/left at the corner, etc.). Write the phrases on the board. In pairs, students look at the maps.

They take turns giving directions to all the unlabeled buildings (the circles). Partners follow the directions.

Also see the Strategy Exercise on page 33.

Culture corner

1. After students have read the Culture Corner, have them answer the question in pairs or small groups: *How do you give directions in your language?*

2. (Optional) After students have read the Culture Corner and understand the English use of "please," dictate the following sentences. If "please" is used correctly, they should write the sentences as they hear them. If "please" is used incorrectly, they should leave it out of the sentence. (Mistakes are underlined.)

1. <u>Please</u> go straight. (Students write, "Go straight.")
2. Please meet me at the video store.
3. Tell me how to get there, please.
4. <u>Please</u> turn left at the drug store.
5. After the restaurant, <u>please</u> turn left.
6. Please come here.

(Sentences 2, 3, and 6 are correct.)

Optional activity

(For use anytime during or after the unit.)

• *Let's take a picture.* Divide the class into an even number of small groups of five to eight students. The groups should work together to arrange themselves according to any principle they like (a line from youngest to oldest, a representation of where they live in relation to each other, etc.). Another group looks at the arrangement and tries to guess the principle. They can ask questions but only get three guesses at the answer.

Listening Task 2
Safari Park

> **Listening skill:** Identifying locations

1. T: *Look at page 35.*

2. (Optional) Read the title: *"Safari Park."* *What do you think this will be about?* Elicit answers from the students. (Answer: the locations of parts of a zoo)

3. (Optional) If your students find listening very challenging, do the Additional Support procedure below.

4. Read the instructions: *Safari Park is a zoo. There are no cages. Listen to the tour of Safari Park. Where are the places? Write the numbers on the map, 1 through 6. There is one extra place on the map.*

5. Play Listening Task 2 on the tape. Gesture for students to write the numbers.

6. (Optional) To make sure students understand what to do, stop after one or two items. Ask students: *Where's Monkey Mountain?* (Answer: between the North American Prairie and Bear Country) *Where's the Children's Zoo?* (Answer: between Bear Country and the Craft Center) Then play the rest of Listening Task 2.

7. If necessary, play Listening Task 2 a second time. Before replaying the tape, you may want to have students compare their answers in pairs: *Work with a partner. Look at your partner's answers. How many were the same? Then we'll listen again.*

8. Check by drawing a quick sketch of the map on the board. Have students call out their answers. (Answers appear in blue on the opposite page.)

ADDITIONAL SUPPORT Have students do the activity in pairs. They use only one book. Have them follow the tours by tracing the route on the map with their fingers. (Also see the Strategy Exercise on page 33.)

NOTES

• A children's zoo is a section of a zoo that features animals that are not dangerous. Children can pet them. Common animals in children's zoos are rabbits and sheep.

• This park is not a real one. However, the activity is based on features of a number of parks including the St. Louis Zoo (St. Louis, Missouri, U.S.A.), The Great Plains Zoo (Sioux Falls, South Dakota, U.S.A.), and Tohoku Safari Park (Fukushima Prefecture, Japan).

Your turn to talk

1. Divide the class into groups of three. T: *Work in groups of three. Start from your school. Describe how to get from your school to someplace nearby. Partners, draw a map. If you don't understand, ask questions. Who can guess the place first?*

2. (Optional) Demonstrate by describing a location yourself while students try to guess.

LISTENING TASK 2

Safari Park

Safari Park is a zoo. There are no cages.

❑ Listen to the tour of Safari Park. Where are the places?
Write the numbers on the map (1–6). There is one extra place on the map.

1. The Life Science Center
2. The Brazilian Rain Forest
3. The Children's Zoo
4. Monkey Mountain
5. Lion Land
6. The Gift Shop

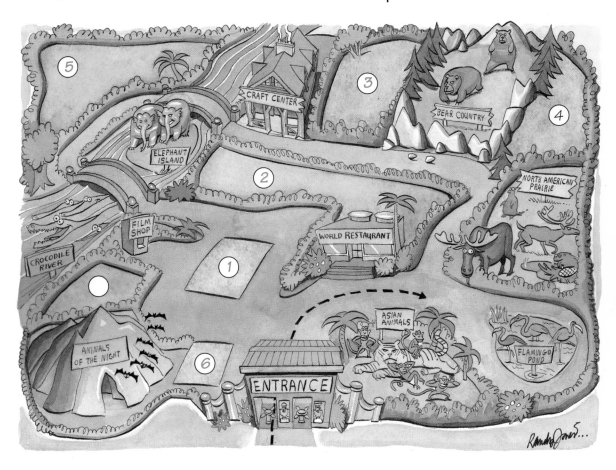

YOUR TURN TO TALK

Work in groups of three. Start from your school. Describe how to get from your school to someplace nearby. Partners, draw a map. If you don't understand the directions, ask questions. Who can guess the place first?

Example: Go out the front door. Turn right. Go straight ahead for two blocks. . . .

35

The Midnight Special

WARMING UP

You will hear a traditional American song.
The song is about a man. He's in jail.
The Midnight Special is a train.
The man can see it and hear it
   from the jail.
He wants the train to take
   him to freedom.

❑ Work with a partner.
   Match the words to the pictures.

1. to arrest someone   4. Houston   7. straw hat
2. bell   5. pan   8. umbrella
3. to gamble   6. sheriff

8

1

2

4

3

7

5

6

U N I T   1 1
The Midnight Special

Topic/function: Enjoying a folk song
Listening skills: Understanding a song,
  identifying a sequence of events
  (Listening Task 1); identifying word
  stress (Listening Task 2)
Grammar/vocabulary: Word stress

Warming Up

1. Hold your book so that students can see
page 36. T: *Look at page 36.*

2. Read the introduction as the students
follow along in their books:

  You will hear a traditional American song.
  The song is about a man. He's in jail.
  The Midnight Special is a train.
  The man can see it and hear it from the jail.
  He wants the train to take him to freedom.

3. Read the task instructions. Pause when
you see the symbol ♦ to give students time
to write.

  Work with a partner.
  Match the words to the pictures. ♦

4. As students work, circulate and help
pairs having difficulty. Some of the
vocabulary may be new to some students.
If there are words they don't know,
encourage the students to skip them. If
they do those they know first, they may be
able to figure out the new words.

5. Check by calling out the words and
having students point to the right pictures
in their books. OR Draw nine squares on
the board to represent the nine pictures.
Have students call out the words for each
picture. (Answers appear in blue on the
opposite page.)

NOTE

• Useful books giving ideas for using song
in class include *Music and Song* by T.
Murphey (Oxford University Press),
Musical Openings by D. Cranmer and C.
Laroy (Longman), and *Songs in Action* by
D. Griffee (Prentice Hall).

Strategy exercise: Looking for
opportunities to listen

Pop songs in English are very popular with
students. They provide an important and
enjoyable opportunity for listening to
English outside of class. Students can do a
class project in which they work in teams
to make lists of radio stations that play
English songs and that have any special
programs, lists of upcoming movies or TV
shows about popular music, or any
supplementary books they would
recommend.

Optional activities

(For use anytime during or after the unit.)

• *Story of a song.* Students work in small
groups to tell each other the stories of
songs they know.

• *Sharing our songs.* In multicultural
classes, students can bring in songs from
their countries and explain the songs to
their classmates. In monocultural classes,
students can share their favorite songs
and, if the songs are not in English, they
can make English summaries of them.

Listening Task 1 What's the story?

Listening skills: Understanding a song, identifying a sequence of events

Note: The tapescript for Unit 11 begins on page T16.

1. T: *Look at page 37.*

2. (Optional) Read the title: *"What's the story?" What do you think this will be about?* Elicit answers from the students. (Answer: the story the song tells)

3. (Optional) If your students find listening very challenging, do the Additional Support procedure below.

4. Read the instructions: *Listen to the song. Number the pictures, one through four.*

5. Play Listening Task 1 on the tape. Gesture for students to number the pictures.

6. If necessary, play Listening Task 1 a second time. If you do, you may want to have students work in pairs to compare their answers before they listen again.

7. Check by drawing four squares on the board to represent the four pictures. Have students call out their answers. (Answers appear in blue on the opposite page.)

ADDITIONAL SUPPORT Write the key words (those in the Warming Up plus any others you think will be new to the students) on paper or index cards (13 x 18 cm./ 5 x 7 in.). You'll need one set for every four students. Students work in groups of four. They close their books and spread the cards randomly on a desk, with the words showing face up. Play the song once. As students listen, they try to hear the target words. When they hear one, each student should be the first to try to touch the word card.

Note: In large classes, it may be too time-consuming to make the necessary sets of cards. Instead, dictate the words and have each group make one set of cards.

NOTES

• The piece of paper in Miss Rosy's hand (verse 3) is probably proof that she has "posted bail." In the United States, when someone is arrested, they can often post bail (pay an amount of money) to be released before they go to trial. The money is a guarantee that the person will appear at the trial.

• Passenger trains in the United States often have names. Two of the most famous are "The Twentieth Century Limited" (New York to Chicago) and "The City of New Orleans" (Chicago to New Orleans). "The Midnight Special" is probably not the official name of the train. Rather, it is a slang name the prisoners use to refer to the train they hear every night.

Culture corner

1. After students have read the Culture Corner, have them answer the questions in pairs or small groups: *Think about folk songs from your country. Are any of the topics the same? What other topics are common?*

2. (Optional) After students have read the Culture Corner, have them brainstorm a list of common themes in folk songs in their country. They then try to identify as many songs as possible that include two or more of the listed themes.

NOTES

• A song that deals with most of the themes listed is "You never even called me by my name (The Perfect Country and Western Song)" written by Steve Goodman and performed by David Allan Coe on *David Allan Coe's Greatest Hits* (Columbia Records).

• You might want to prepare for Listening Task 2 by doing a word stress activity with this Culture Corner. See instruction number 2 in the Culture Corner plan for Unit 17 (page 55).

LISTENING TASK 1

What's the story?

❏ Listen to the song.
Number the pictures (1–4).

2

4

3

1

 CULTURE CORNER

Folk songs are traditional songs that most people in a country know. They learn the words from their friends and family. Sometimes the words to these songs change over time. Many folk songs have similar topics and words. In American and Canadian folk music, these are some of the most common topics:

- problems with love
- problems with life
- traveling
- jail or prison

- family, especially the mother
- rain
- crying
- hope for the future

Think about folk songs from your country. Are any of the topics the same? What other topics are common?

37

LISTENING TASK 2
Catch the rhythm.

❑ Listen to the song again.
   <u>Underline</u> the stressed (loudest) syllables.

Oh, <u>let</u> the <u>Midnight</u> <u>Special</u>
<u>Shine</u> a <u>light</u> on <u>me</u>.
Oh, <u>let</u> the <u>Midnight</u> <u>Special</u>
<u>Shine</u> an <u>ever-lov</u>ing <u>light</u> on <u>me</u>.

1. <u>If</u> you <u>ever</u> <u>get</u> to <u>Houston</u>,
   You'd <u>better</u> act <u>right</u>.
   You'd <u>better</u> not <u>gamble</u>,
   And you'd <u>better</u> not <u>fight</u>.
   The <u>sheriff</u> will ar<u>rest</u> <u>you</u>.
   He's <u>going</u> to <u>take</u> you <u>down</u>.*
   The <u>next</u> thing you <u>know</u> is
   That you're <u>jailhouse</u> <u>bound</u>.

(Chorus)

2. Every <u>Monday</u> <u>morning</u>
   <u>When</u> the <u>big</u> bell <u>rings</u>,
   You <u>go</u> to the <u>table</u>,
   You <u>see</u> the <u>same</u> old <u>things</u>.
   <u>Not</u> much <u>food</u> on the <u>table</u>,
   <u>Just</u> some <u>bread</u> in a <u>pan</u>.
   If you say <u>anything</u> a<u>bout</u> <u>it</u>,
   You <u>get</u> in <u>trouble</u> with the <u>man</u>.**

(Chorus)

3. <u>Here</u> comes <u>Miss</u> <u>Rosy</u>.
   Oh, <u>how</u> can you <u>tell</u>?
   By the umbrella on her <u>shoulder</u>,
   She's <u>such</u> a good-<u>looking</u> <u>gal</u>.
   A straw <u>hat</u> is on her <u>head</u>,
   <u>Piece</u> of <u>paper</u> in her <u>hand</u>.
   She <u>wants</u> to see the <u>jailer</u>,
   She <u>wants</u> to free her <u>man</u>.

(Chorus)

*take you down = put you in jail
  This is an uncommon expression.

**the man = the sheriff

YOUR TURN TO TALK

First, sing the song. Then snap your fingers or tap the desk. As a group, read the first verse in rhythm. Try to match the stressed syllables to the rhythm. Finally, work with a partner. Try to read the whole song in rhythm. One person keeps time. (Snap your fingers or tap the desk in an even beat.) The other person reads. Then change parts.

Listening Task 2
Catch the rhythm.

Listening skill: Identifying word stress

1. T: *Look at page 38.*

2. (Optional) Read the title: *"Catch the rhythm." What do you think this will be about?* Elicit answers from the students. (Answer: identifying rhythm/word stress)

3. (Optional) If your students find listening very challenging, do the Additional Support procedure below.

4. Read the instructions: *Listen to the song again. Underline the stressed (loudest) syllables.*

5. Play Listening Task 2 on the tape. Gesture for students to underline the stressed syllables.

6. (Optional) To make sure students understand what to do, stop after the first verse. Read the verse aloud. Have students snap their figures or tap the desk on the stressed syllable.

7. If necessary, play Listening Task 2 a second time. Before replaying the tape, you may want to have students compare their answers in pairs: *Work with a partner. Look at the syllables your partner underlined. Were they the same? Then we'll listen again.*

8. Check by reading the song aloud. Students snap their fingers or tap their desks on the stressed syllable. (Stress is marked in blue on the opposite page.)

ADDITIONAL SUPPORT Have students read along silently as you play the song. As they read, they snap their fingers or tap their desks or feet in rhythm. The physical movement will help them "feel" the rhythm.

NOTES

• Make sure students understand the meaning of "syllable." One good way is to contrast a few words as you clap your

hands to show each syllable. Possible words: Syllable (3), rhythm (2), underline (3), Midnight (2).

• Stress and timing are a key feature of English. English is a stress-timed language. This means the stresses tend to come at equal intervals. Other, unstressed words are "squeezed" between. This lesson helps students become more aware of the rhythm of English. This is particularly important for students who speak syllable-timed languages where each syllable takes about the same amount of time to say.

• "The Midnight Special" has been recorded by many different artists in a variety of styles including rock and country. As a follow-up, students often enjoy hearing another version.

Your turn to talk

1. T: *Stand up. Let's sing the song.*

2. (after they've sung the song) T: *Read the first verse in rhythm. Try to match the stressed syllables to the rhythm.* (Snap your fingers to help them keep in rhythm.)

3. T: *Now, work with a partner. Try to read the whole song in rhythm. One person keeps time. The other person reads. Then change parts.*

NOTE

• If you have access to a metronome, it may be useful for Step 2 of the Your Turn to Talk activity plan.

Optional activity

(For use anytime after students have done Listening Task 2).

• *Song parody.* Students work in small groups to change the words of "The Midnight Special" to a song about their school. They might start with:

"If you ever come to our school,
You'd better . . ."

U N I T 1 2

Gifts and greetings

Topic/function: Describing gifts and
greetings in different countries
Listening skills: Identifying reasons
(Listening Task 1); identifying customs
(Listening Task 2)
Grammar/vocabulary: Negative imperatives
(*Don't . . .*), *You shouldn't . . .*

Warming Up

I. Hold your book so that students can see
page 39. T: *Look at page 39.*

2. Read the instructions. Pause when you
see the symbol ♦ to give students time to
answer the questions.

> *Work with a partner.*
> *Answer the questions.* ♦

3. (Optional) Choose one of the questions
that is likely to produce a variety of
answers. Ask the question (e.g., *What kinds
of gifts do you give when you go to a friend's
wedding?*) and, as a full class, brainstorm
possible answers.

4. As students work, circulate and help
pairs having difficulty.

5. Check by reading the questions and
having students call out their answers.

6. Ask one or two students the questions at
the bottom of the page. *Are there any gifts in
your country that have a bad meaning? Which
gifts?*

NOTES

• An alternate way of doing the activity is
as a match game. Students first answer
individually. Then they work in groups of
three. Each time they write the same
answer as someone else, they get a point.

• If there are any situations students
don't know the answers for (for example, a
business meeting), they should write what
they think is typical or "I don't know."

• The question about business meetings
was included to bring out cultural
information. In some cultures, gifts are an
accepted and expected part of doing
business. In other cultures, they are seen
as bribes and should be avoided.

Strategy exercise: *Positive statements*

By now, students are more than halfway
through the book. They may feel restless
with the school term and in need of
encouragement. Now would be a good
time to review the goals you talked about
at the beginning of the course and see how
much progress has been made. Students
should think of one positive thing they
have accomplished or one activity they
really enjoyed or did well. They may prefer
not to say which it is. It is adequate to have
them think about it or write it down. Stress
the positive, and the importance of not
getting discouraged in language learning.

Optional activities

(For use anytime during or after the unit.)

• *Unusual gifts.* Students work in small
groups to describe the most unusual gifts
they have ever received. They should
answer the following questions:

1. What was it?
2. Who gave it to you?
3. When did you get it?
4. Where did you get it?
5. Why did you get it?

Partners should ask one follow-up question
for each *Wh-* question.

• *Meet the UFO!* Tell students they are
going to greet a UFO filled with aliens who
do not understand English. How will they
pantomime greetings and teach other
gestures they will need to communicate?
Once they decide in their groups, they
should teach another group, which must
remain silent.

Gifts and greetings

❑ Work with a partner.
Answer the questions.

Gift Survey

What kinds of gifts do you give when . . . SAMPLE ANSWERS

1. you go to a friend's wedding? _money_

2. you visit a friend or stay with
a family in another country? _food from your country_

3. you celebrate a friend's birthday? _a cake_

4. you go to a business meeting? _a calendar_

5. you want to give something
to someone you love? _roses_

❑ Are there any gifts in your country that have
a bad meaning? Which gifts?

Gifts and cultures

People in all countries enjoy gifts.
Sometimes the meanings are different in other cultures.

❑ Listen. Which item is not a good gift? Cross out (X) the picture.
Why not? Check (✔) your answer.

1. China

✔ A handkerchief means "goodbye."
☐ Dinner costs too much.

2. Argentina

✔ A tie is too personal.
☐ Plants are bad luck.

3. Switzerland

☐ Candy isn't healthy.
✔ Roses mean love.

4. Italy

✔ Even numbers (2, 4, 6, 8, 10) are unlucky.
☐ Odd numbers (1, 3, 5, 7, 9) are unlucky.

5. Japan

☐ Pen and pencil sets are unpopular.
✔ "Four" sounds like the word for "death."

CULTURE CORNER

In many countries, people give special gifts at certain times. Sometimes the customs seem unusual:

• In Australia, a birthday cake for a 21-year-old is often shaped like a key. It means the person is an adult and can come home at any time.
• In parts of Africa, people give a cow as a wedding present.
• Before Korean students take university entrance tests, their friends give them sticky rice candy for luck. The friends hope that the students will pass the test and go to the university.

When do people in your country give gifts? Are there any gifts that people from other countries might find unusual?

Listening Task 1
Gifts and cultures

Listening skill: Identifying reasons

Note: The tapescript for Unit 12 begins on page T16.

1. T: *Look at page 40.*

2. (Optional) Read the title: *"Gifts and cultures." What do you think this will be about?* Elicit answers from the students. (Answer: gifts that are and are not appropriate in various cultures)

3. (Optional) If your students find listening very challenging, do the Additional Support procedure below.

4. Read the instructions: *Listen. Which item is not a good gift? Cross out the picture. Why not? Check your answer.*

5. Play Listening Task 1 on the tape. Gesture for students to cross out the pictures and check their answers.

6. (Optional) To make sure students understand what to do, stop after the second item. Ask students: *Which did you check?* (Answer: a tie, because it is too personal) Then play the rest of Listening Task 1.

7. If necessary, play Listening Task 1 a second time.

8. Check by having students call out their answers. (Answers appear in blue on the opposite page.)

ADDITIONAL SUPPORT Have students look at the reasons below each item. In pairs, they guess which answer is true. Of course, there is no reason that the students "should" already know the correct answers. However, the process of guessing will make them familiar with the choices. Also, having guessed, students will often focus their listening to see if they were right.

NOTES

• These cultural "rules" are generalizations for the countries. Of course, individuals may act differently.

• The Japanese word referred to in item 5 is "shi." Depending on the character used, it can mean either "four" or "death."

• Much of the information in this unit came from *Do's and Taboos Around the World, Second Edition* (1990) and *Gestures* (1991), both by Roger E. Axtell (New York: John Wiley and Sons). The information about handkerchiefs in Chinese culture was learned by one of the authors the hard way; he gave handkerchiefs as gifts to several Taiwan Chinese friends. The authors strongly recommend learning about gift-giving customs before people visit other cultures.

Culture corner

1. After students have read the Culture Corner, have them answer the questions in pairs or small groups: *When do people in your country give gifts? Are there any gifts that people from other countries might find unusual?*

2. (Optional) Before class, make copies of the Culture Corner. On the copies, delete the names of the places. In class, distribute the copies. Individually or in pairs, students guess the countries. Then they read the Culture Corner in the book to see if they were correct.

NOTE

• The "sticky" rice candy expresses the hope that students will "stick to" the university (become connected with it).

Optional activity

(For use anytime after students have done Listening Task 1.)

• *In my country* . . . Students work in pairs or small groups. They write the script for a conversation similar to those in Listening Task 1 for their own country.

Listening Task 2
Greetings around the world

Listening skill: Identifying customs

1. T: *Look at page 41.*

2. (Optional) Read the title: *"Greetings around the world." What do you think this will be about?* Elicit answers from the students. (Answer: different ways to greet people in other cultures)

3. (Optional) If your students find listening very challenging, do the Additional Support procedure below.

4. Read the instructions: *Listen. There are many ways to greet people. These are a few examples from some countries. Draw lines from the greetings to the places. Each has two answers.*

5. Play Listening Task 1 on the tape. Gesture for students to draw lines to the countries.

6. (Optional) To make sure students understand what to do, stop after the second item. Ask students: *Where do people hug?* (Answer: Russia, Brazil) Then play the rest of Listening Task 2.

7. If necessary, play Listening Task 2 a second time.

8. Check by saying the names of the greetings and having students call out their answers. (Answers appear in blue on the opposite page.)

ADDITIONAL SUPPORT Have students close their books. Play the tape one time. Each time they hear the name of a country or nationality, they raise their hands. OR Have students work in pairs. With their partners, they try all six greetings. They may want to think about what, if anything, they feel as they do the action. The purpose of trying the actions is to make them familiar with the content they are listening for.

NOTES

• The hand gesture used for a "namaste" or "wai" looks similar to the gesture many cultures use for prayer. According to anthropologist Joseph Campbell, this grows out of a cultural tradition of acknowledging the goodness in the person one is greeting.

• Traditionally, Japanese bows where the left hand covers the right hand are more polite than when the right hand covers the left. This is because, in the days when people used swords, the right hand was used for fighting. The left hand covering the right symbolizes one's stopping one's own stronger hand. Some companies such as airlines still teach their employees to bow in this way.

• You may prefer to check after each item rather than waiting until students have heard all six parts.

Your turn to talk

1. Divide the class into groups of three. T: *Work in groups of three. What gifts are typical of your country or area? Make a list of five gifts.*

2. (after about five minutes) T: *Now join another group. Combine your lists. Choose the three best gifts.*

3. At the end, you may want a few groups to present their lists to the whole class.

NOTES

• If you are teaching students from a variety of countries, have them make the list of gifts from the country they are now in. The list includes things they would give to people in the countries they are from.

• An interesting variation of this activity is to have students select gifts that will help a person new to the country understand the culture. To make it slightly more challenging, make a rule that only one of the items can be a book.

LISTENING TASK 2

Identifying customs

Greetings around the world

❏ Listen. There are many ways to greet people. These are a few examples from some countries.
Draw lines from the greetings to the places. Each has two answers.

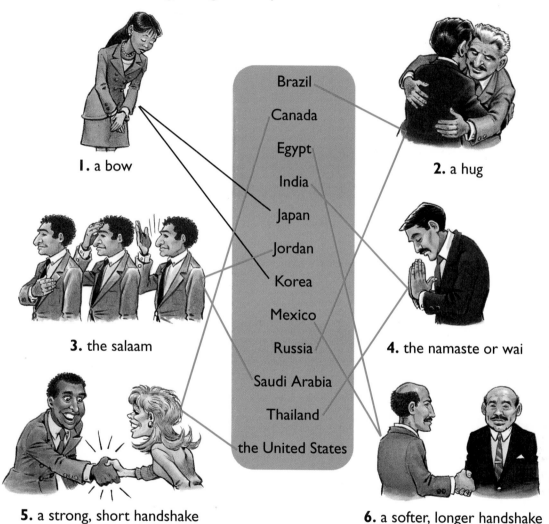

1. a bow

2. a hug

3. the salaam

4. the namaste or wai

5. a strong, short handshake

6. a softer, longer handshake

Brazil
Canada
Egypt
India
Japan
Jordan
Korea
Mexico
Russia
Saudi Arabia
Thailand
the United States

YOUR TURN TO **TALK**

Work in groups of three. What gifts are typical of your country or area? Make a list of five gifts. Then join another group. Combine your lists. Choose the three best gifts. Give opinions like this:

_____ is typical (in my country).

How about _____ ? It's popular (in my country).

Time changes everything.

❏ Work with a partner.
Do you know these jobs?
Write the numbers in the boxes.

1. ambulance driver
2. bodybuilder
3. carpenter
4. factory worker
5. gas station attendant
6. pop musician
7. porter
8. store clerk
9. teacher

8

9

2

6

1

4

7

3

5

❏ Now look at the pictures on page 43.
Before they became famous, these people each had one of the jobs above.
What jobs do you think they had?
Write their old jobs.

UNIT 13
Time changes everything.

> ***Topic/function:*** Talking about what people
> did when they were younger
> ***Listening skills:*** Identifying jobs (Listening
> Task 1); understanding personal
> information questions (Listening Task 2)
> ***Grammar/vocabulary:*** Past with *used to*,
> names of jobs and occupations

Warming Up

1. Hold your book so that students can see
page 42. T: *Look at page 42.*

2. Read the instructions. Pause when you
see the symbol ♦ to give students time to
answer the questions.

> *Work with a partner.*
> *Do you know these jobs?*
> *Write the numbers in the boxes.* ♦

3. Allow a few minutes for students to
work. Then check by drawing nine squares
on the board in the pattern of the
pictures. Ask about each job: *Which picture
is the ambulance driver?* (Answers appear in
blue on the opposite page.)

4. Continue with the instructions at the
bottom of the page:

> *Now look at the pictures on page 43.*
> *Before they became famous, these people each*
> *had one of the jobs above.*
> *What jobs do you think they had?*
> *Write their old jobs.* ♦

5. As students work, circulate. Encourage
students to guess, even when they aren't
sure.

6. Since they will find out if their guesses
were correct after they have done
Listening Task 1, it isn't necessary to check
at this time.

NOTES

• The pictures of the people in the
various occupations are intended to
establish meaning of the vocabulary. The
sex and race of the people in pictures
shouldn't be taken as hints as to which
entertainer used to do each job.

• *Used to + BE* (She used to be a singer.)
and *used to* + infinitive (He used to work at
a gas station.) are used only to talk about
situations in the past that are no longer
true. Note that this is different from *BE +
used to* (He is used to this city now.) which
means "accustomed to."

Strategy exercise: Reviewing

Talking about the past leads naturally to
reviewing. Students can always profit from
review. A useful review technique is
"spiraling." Spiraling means reviewing
material on the day you learn it, then the
next day, then two days later, then at ever-
increasing intervals (but always reviewing).
The key is putting the information into a
variety of contexts (new sentences,
associations, etc.). Different systems of
review work for different learners.
Encourage students to learn some new
ways of reviewing from their peers and to
try at least one new way this week.

Optional activity

(For use anytime during or after the unit.)

• ***To tell the truth.*** Students work in groups
of three. They each tell about an unusual
experience that happened to them. The
group decides on one experience. Then
they join a new group. They each pretend
the experience happened to them. They
each briefly tell about the experience and
partners ask questions and try to decide
who really had the experience.

Listening Task 1
What did they use to do?

Listening skill: Identifying jobs

Note: The tapescript for Unit 13 begins on page T18.

1. T: *Look at pages 42 and 43 .*

2. Read the title: *"What did they use to do?" Now we'll find out which entertainers really did these jobs.*

3. **(Optional)** If your students find listening very challenging, do the Additional Support procedure below.

4. Read the instructions: *Listen. Did you guess the old jobs correctly? Correct your answers.*

5. Play Listening Task 1 on the tape. Gesture for students to correct mistaken guesses.

6. **(Optional)** To make sure students understand what to do, stop after the second item. Ask: *What did Whoopi Goldberg use to do?* (Answer: She was a teacher.) T: *If you made a different guess, cross it out. If you guessed the answer correctly, don't do anything.* Then play the rest of Listening Task 1.

7. If necessary, play Listening Task 1 a second time.

8. Check by saying the names of the entertainers. Students call out the jobs. (Answers appear in blue on the opposite page.)

ADDITIONAL SUPPORT Have students do this listening task in pairs. Each pair uses only one book. OR Have them put one book between them. They fold the book so it is open to the Warming Up page (p. 42). Students listen to the tape once. Partners race to be the first to touch the picture of each job as it is mentioned.

NOTES

• To increase the game-like feeling of this activity, you may want to stop the tape before each item and have students call out their guesses. Have the other students raise their hands to see how many agree.

• The information in this activity came from a variety of sources including *The Cambridge Biographical Encyclopedia* (1994) by D. Crystal (Cambridge), T*he Book of Lists 3* (1983) by D. Wallenchinsky, I. Wallace, & A. Wallace (Corgi), and *Reaching for the Stars* (1991) by R. Hernandez (Eishosha Longman).

Culture corner

1. After students have read the Culture Corner, have them answer the questions in pairs or small groups: *Do famous people in your country use stage/pen names? Do you know their real names?*

2. **(Optional)** Before students have read the Culture Corner, have them close their books. Read the Culture Corner to them twice. Students then work in pairs. They write as much as they remember. It isn't necessary for them to remember exactly what you said, just the basic meaning. After they have been working about five minutes, read the Culture Corner again to check. When they've finished, they read the Culture Corner on page 43. They underline everything on the page that was included in what they wrote.

You may want to add a step where each pair joins another pair. They exchange papers and make any corrections they can in content, grammar, or spelling.

NOTE

• The activity in Step 2 above is based loosely on the Dictogloss Technique. For more information on Dictogloss, see *Grammar Dictation* by Ruth Wajnryb (Oxford University Press).

 **LISTENING TASK 1**

What did they use to do?

❑ Listen. Did you guess the old jobs correctly?
Correct your answers.

1. Arnold Schwarzenegger
bodybuilder

2. Whoopi Goldberg
teacher

3. Walt Disney
ambulance driver

4. Michelle Pfeiffer
store clerk

5. Harrison Ford
carpenter

6. Bette Midler
factory worker

7. Sean Connery
porter

8. Cher
pop musician

9. Clint Eastwood
gas station attendant

 CULTURE CORNER

In many countries, some entertainers and writers do not use their real names.
They use "stage names" (entertainers) or "pen names" (writers):

Stage/pen name	*Real name*
Mark Twain (author)	Samuel Clemens
Ringo Starr (musician)	Richard Starkey
Cher (actress)	Cherilyn LaPiere

Do famous people in your country use stage/pen names? Do you know their real names?

When I was younger . . .

❏ Listen. What did you use to do when you were a child?
Write the missing words in the circles.
Then complete the sentences about yourself.

EXAMPLE ANSWERS

1. When I was a child, I used to (go to school) _by bus_____.

2. (During holidays), I used to go _to the beach_____.

3. (After school), I used to _play with my friends_____.

4. (A game) I used to play was _baseball_____.

5. My favorite (TV show) used to be _The Cosby Show_____.

6. (My hair) used to be _longer_____.

7. (At school) I used to dislike _math_____.

8. (The season) I used to like the most was _summer_____.

Work with a partner. Read your answers to Listening Task 2. Listen to your partner's answers. Ask at least one question about each answer. Try to learn at least three new things about your partner. How often did you write the same answers?

Example
A: When I was a child, I used to go to school by bus.
B: How long did it take? OR Who did you go with? . . .

Listening Task 2
When I was younger . . .

Listening skill: Understanding personal information questions

1. T: *Look at page 44.*

2. (Optional) Read the title: "*When I was younger . . .*" *What do you think this will be about?* Elicit answers from the students. (Answer: personalized information about the students)

3. Read the instructions: *Listen. What did you do when you were a child? Write the missing words in the circles. Then complete the sentences about yourself.*

4. Play Listening Task 1 on the tape. Gesture for students to finish the sentences. Note that they should complete the sentences as they do each item, rather than waiting until the end, after they have done all the dictation.

5. (Optional) If your students find listening very challenging, do the Additional Support procedure below.

6. (Optional) To make sure students understand what to do, stop after the first item. Ask two or three students: *How did you used to go to school?* Encourage several answers. Then play the rest of Listening Task 2, stopping between items to allow more writing time if necessary.

7. If necessary, play Listening Task 2 a second time.

8. Students will go though all the items when they do Your Turn to Talk. If you feel it is necessary to check now, have them dictate the sentences back to you as you write them on the board. (Answers appear in blue on the opposite page.)

ADDITIONAL SUPPORT Do each item in two parts: The first section which sets up the topic and the second section which is a dictation. Play the first section, twice if necessary. Have students work in small groups. They talk about what they understood. They call out their ideas. You confirm if they are correct. Then play the second section. Students do the dictation and complete the sentences about themselves. Continue for each item.

NOTE

• Although Step 6 of the lesson plan suggests pausing the tape to allow more time for writing, don't stop for too long. Part of the activity is to encourage fluency.

Your turn to talk

1. Divide the class into pairs. T: *Work with a partner. Read your answers to Listening Task 2. Listen to your partner's answers. Ask at least one question about each answer. Try to learn at least three new things about your partner. How often did you write the same answers?*

2. (Optional) Demonstrate asking different follow-up questions. Ask one student: *How did you use to go to school?* After the student answers, elicit various follow-up questions from the class. (Examples: How long did it take? Who did you go with? Did you ever go a different way? Was it difficult in the winter?)

Optional activity

(For use anytime during or after the unit.)

• ***Pantomime vacations.*** Work with the whole class to brainstorm a list of action verbs related to things people do on vacations. The students work in pairs. They pantomime the story of a vacation (real or imagined). The partner can ask questions, but the mime cannot speak; the mime can only nod "yes" or "no." A variation is to have the pairs join into groups of four. The pair members tell the new partners about the vacation they just learned about.

UNIT 14
Can you describe it?

Topic/function: Describing people, things, and events

Listening skills: Understanding descriptions of people and things (Listening Tasks 1); understanding descriptions of events (Listening Task 2)

Grammar/vocabulary: Descriptive adjectives

Warming Up

1. Hold your book so that students can see page 45. T: *Look at page 45.*

2. Read the following instructions. Pause when you see the symbol ♦ to give students time to write.

> *Look at each word.*
> *Write a word with the opposite meaning.*
> *There is more than one correct answer.*
> *For example, the opposite of "right" could be "wrong" or it could be "left."* ♦

3. As students work, circulate and help pairs having difficulty.

4. When they finish writing, read the instructions at the bottom of the page:

> *Work with a partner. Play a game.*
> *Say your answers.*
> *Listen to your partner's answers.*
> *If you wrote the same word, you each get one point. If you wrote different words with the same meaning, you get two points. If you wrote different words with different meanings, you get three points.*

5. (Optional) Demonstrate the activity by directing one pair through the first two or three items. Make it clear how many points they get for each answer.

6. As they work, circulate and help pairs having difficulty.

7. It isn't necessary to check answers, but it can be useful to call out the words and see how many different opposites students thought of.

NOTES

• You may want to precede the activity with a review of what "opposite" means. Ask for the opposites of a few simple words (*hot, black, happy,* etc.).

• This unit deals with descriptions, so students are working with adjectives. In English sentences, adjectives occur in the following order: 1. size, 2. shape, 3. age, 4. color, 5. nationality/origin (where something comes from), 6. material (what something is made of), and 7. purpose (what it is for). (Example: a big, square, old, brown, German, wooden writing desk)

Strategy exercise: Getting ideas quickly

Listening Task 1 presents two different tasks. Students listen to get a general idea of the message and decide which picture is correct. They also write the words that helped them understand. It is not always easy to clearly divide types of listening. Remind students that they listen for a purpose and point out that they should use the directions or the situation to help them decide why they are listening. This will focus their attention, and they will understand more quickly than they could by trying to get all the information.

Optional activity

(For use anytime during or after the unit.)

• *A big, old, yellow Chinese vase.* Put the order of adjectives on the board (see the last note above). Either have students contribute one object each, or bring in a bag of interesting objects yourself. Work in as many teams as you have board space for. Show an object to the first person on each team. That person is responsible for writing a description of the object, with help from teammates, who may speak but cannot write. The team with the longest and best description wins. You will probably have to supply the noun.

Can you describe it?

❑ Look at each word.
Write a word with the opposite meaning.
There is more than one correct answer.

SAMPLE
ANSWERS

1. right   _____wrong_____ **OR** _____left_____

2. old   *new*   *young*

3. hard   *soft*   *easy*

4. light   *dark*   *heavy*

5. cheap   *expensive*   *good (high quality)*

6. smart   *stupid*   *unfashionable*

7. sweet   *sour*   *unkind*

8. dull   *interesting*   *sharp*

9. narrow   *wide*   *open-minded*

❑ Work with a partner. Play a game.
Say your answers.
Listen to your partner's answers.

- Same word = 1 point.
- Different words with the same meaning
  (*wrong/incorrect*) = 2 points.
- Different words with different meanings
  (*wrong/left*) = 3 points.

Your points: _____

Which one?

❏ Listen. What are the people describing?
Check (✔) the correct pictures.
How did you know? Write the words.

1.

☐   ✔

chocolate, dirty face, cute

2.

✔   ☐

love story, happy

3.

✔   ☐

dark, plain

4.

☐   ✔

strange, tall, narrow, road winds

5.

☐   ✔

mysterious, ugly, scary

6.

✔   ☐

happy, smiling, laughing

CULTURE CORNER

One of the most common ways to describe something is by its color. But not every language has the same color names. For example, Navaho, spoken by some Native Americans, uses the same word for blue and green. Russian has two words for different kinds of blue: *sinij* and *goluboj.* In English, we also have words for different kinds of blue, like "dark blue" and "sky blue." How many different words for colors do you know in English?

Listening Task 1
Which one?

Listening skill: Understanding descriptions of people and things

Note: The tapescript for Unit 14 begins on page T20.

1. T: *Look at page 46.*

2. (Optional) Read the title: *"Which one?" What do you think this will be about?* Elicit answers from the students. (Answer: deciding which picture is being described)

3. (Optional) If your students find listening very challenging, do the Additional Support procedure below.

4. Read the instructions: *Listen. What are the people describing? Check the correct pictures. How did you know? Write the words.*

5. Play Listening Task 1 on the tape. Gesture for students to check the pictures and write the words that gave them the information.

6. (Optional) To make sure students understand what to do, stop after the first item. T: *It's the boy on the right. He has a dirty face. He's cute. What other words gave you the answer?* Elicit suggestions (tall, chocolate, mess). Then play the rest of Listening Task 1.

7. If necessary, play Listening Task 1 a second time. Before replaying it, you may want to have students work together to compare answers and the words that gave them the clues.

8. Check answers by asking: *The picture on the left or the picture on the right? How did you know?* Encourage them to give as many "hint words" as possible. (Answers appear in blue on the opposite page.)

ADDITIONAL SUPPORT Have students work in groups of three. They look at each picture and write two or three adjectives.

They should write the first things that they think of since those items will usually be the main factors in a description.

Culture corner

1. After students have read the Culture Corner, have them answer the question in pairs or small groups: *How many different words for colors do you know in English?*

2. (Optional) After students have read the Culture Corner, have them work in groups of three or four to write out their answers to the question. Write all the words on the board. When new or unusual words come up, give examples of things that are that color. Then students take turns. They think of one of the words and "write it" in the air with their fingers. Partners must figure out what the word is. When they answer, they must give an example along with the name of the color. (Example: A swimming pool is aqua.)

Optional activity

(For use anytime during or after the unit.)

• *One minute each.* Students work in groups of four. Each group consists of two teams with two people each. They put a small object in the middle of the table. The object serves as a buzzer. They must touch the buzzer every time they want to answer. You call out the topics. Teams have one minute to say as many things as possible that fit the description. They get one point for each item.

Topics: Things that are . . .
1. hot	5. purple
2. new	6. sweet
3. light	7. fashionable
4. scary	8. free

Note: The reason for using the "buzzer" is to know which team says a given word first. Their speaking will often overlap, and it makes it harder to keep score.

Listening Task 2
Your story

Listening skill: Understanding descriptions of events

1. T: *Look at page 47.*

2. (Optional) Read the title: *"Your story."* *What do you think this will be about?* Elicit answers from the students. (Answer: making their own version of a story)

3. Read the instructions: *Listen to the story. Imagine the scene.*

4. Play the first part of Listening Task 2 on the tape. **(Optional)** You may want to have students close their eyes to make it easier to imagine the story.

5. (Optional) If your students find listening very challenging, do the Additional Support procedure.

6. Read the second set of instructions: *Listen again. Write the missing words on the lines. When you hear the bell, write any word in the circle that makes sense.*

7. Play the second part of the tape. Gesture for the students to write the missing words and other words they think of.

8. (Optional) To make sure students understand what to do, stop after the first sentence. Ask: *What kind of road?* Encourage several students to give different answers.

9. If necessary, play Listening Task 2 a second time.

10. Students will "check" their additions (the words in the circles) during Your Turn to Talk. To check the other words, read the story, stopping before the missing words. Have students call out their answers. When you come to the circles, tap your desk to represent the bell but don't check those words yet.

ADDITIONAL SUPPORT Have students close their eyes. Instead of playing the first part of the tape, read the script (see page T20 of this manual). Read slowly and clearly. Then read it again. After each sentence, stop and ask students to think about what everything looked like. (Example: *A road went through a forest. What kind of road? What did it look like? Was it straight or winding? Was it narrow or wide? What was the forest like? How big was it?*) After they have a clear image of the story, they return to the taped activity.

Your turn to talk

1. Divide the class into groups of four. T: *Have a "creativity contest." Work in groups of four. Read your stories. Compare the words you wrote when you heard the bell. Whenever someone wrote a word that no one else wrote, he or she gets one point. If everyone wrote different words, each person gets one point.*

2. (Optional) Demonstrate the activity by having each member of one group read their first sentence. Note matches and "creative" answers.

3. (as groups start to finish) T: *Now, finish the story as a group. What happened next?*

4. (Optional) If time permits, you may want to recombine groups and have them share their conclusions.

NOTES

• If available, small objects like poker chips are useful as counters during this activity.

• The "creativity contest" aspect is included to give students a reason to pay attention to what their partners say. To term an answer "creative" simply because only one person wrote it is somewhat arbitrary, but for the sake of the activity, it is effective.

Your story

❏ Listen to the story. Imagine the scene.

❏ Listen again. Write the missing words on the lines.
When you hear the bell, write any word in the circle that makes sense.

SAMPLE
ANSWERS

A (*long*) road went ___*through*___ a (*dark*) ___*forest*___ .

A (*young*) ___*woman*___ was ___*walking*___ down

the ___*road*___ . Suddenly she ___*saw*___ a (*little*) ___*man*___ .

He was ___*wearing*___ a (*red*) ___*shirt*___ ,

(*blue*) ___*pants*___ , and a (*big*) ___*hat*___ .

He ___*smiled*___ and ___*said*___ ,

" *Good morning* ."

YOUR TURN TO

TALK

Creativity Contest. Work in groups of four. Read your stories. Compare the words you wrote when you heard the bell. Whenever someone wrote a word that no one else wrote, he or she gets one point. If everyone wrote different words, each person gets one point. Your points: _____

Finish the story as a group. What happened next?

47

Languages

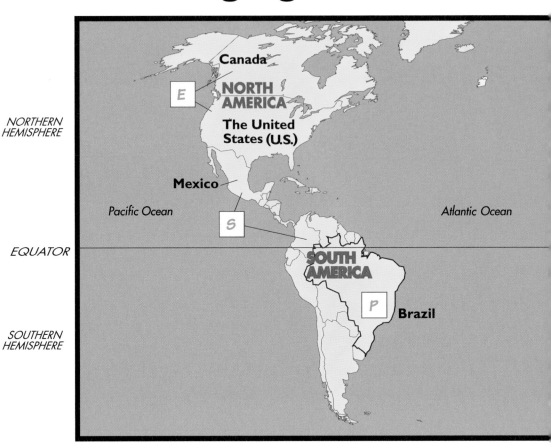

There are probably between 4,000 and 5,000 languages in the world.

❏ Work with a partner.
How many languages can you name in two minutes? Write them.

SAMPLE
ANSWERS

English	Chinese	Russian
Spanish	Portuguese	Greek
Japanese	French	Italian
Korean	Arabic	German

❏ Now join another pair.
Read your list.
Listen to theirs.

U N I T   1 5
Languages

Topic/function: Talking about the
   languages of the world
Listening skills: Identifying countries
   (Listening Task 1); distinguishing types
   of English (Listening Task 2)
Grammar/vocabulary: American and
   British vocabulary and pronunciation
   differences

Warming Up

1. Hold your book so that students can see
page 48. T: *Look at page 48.*
2. Read the introduction and the
instructions. Pause when you see the
symbol ♦ to give students time to answer
the questions.

> There are probably between 4,000 and 5,000
>   languages in the world.
> Work with a partner.
> How many languages can you name in two
>   minutes? Write them. ♦

3. As students work, circulate and help
pairs having difficulty. If pairs can't think
of any beyond the few most common
languages, suggest countries that you think
they'll know the languages of.
4. (Optional) (after 2 minutes) T: *How
many did you write? Which pair got the most?*
5. Read the second set of instructions:

> Now join another pair.
> Read your list.
> Listen to theirs.

6. (Optional) Check answers by having
students call out the languages they wrote.
Count how many the class as a whole listed.

NOTE

• To do this activity as a game, have pairs
keep score at Step 5 of the lesson plan.
They get one point for each language they
wrote that the other pair didn't write.

Strategy exercise: *Contrasting languages*

Teachers sometimes worry whether to let
their students use what they know in their
own language(s). While we do not want to
encourage translation, there is a place for
contrasting languages. Students might
want to talk about dialects of their
language(s) and describe the differences.

Optional activity

(For use anytime during or after the unit.)
• *Language Find Someone Who.* Most
students will already know how to do a
"Find someone who . . . " activity since they
did one as Listening Task 2 of Unit 1. They
stand and circulate. They ask the questions
from the worksheet below. When someone
says "Yes," they write the person's name on
the line. (Possible answers – question 5:
Canada; 6: India)

**Language Find Someone Who . . .
Worksheet**

Ask other students the questions below.
When someone says "Yes," write that
person's name next to the question. Use
each name only one time.

Find someone who . . .
  1. can say "hello" in three languages.
(Can you say . . . ?)
  2. can say "goodbye" in three languages.
  3. can say "thank you" in four languages.
  4. can count to five in another language.
  5. can name a country with two languages.
  6. can name a country with more than
     four languages.
  7. has studied a language other than
     English. (Have you studied . . . ?)
  8. studied English as a child.(Did you
     study . . . ?)
  9. is studying another language now.
     (Are you studying . . . ?)
 10. loves English. (Do you love . . . ?)

© Cambridge University Press

Listening Task I
World languages

Listening skill: Identifying countries

Note: The tapescript for Unit 15 begins on page T20.

I. T: *Look at pages 48 and 49.*

2. (Optional) Read the title: *"World languages." What do you think this will be about?* Elicit answers from the students. (Answer: the most common languages in the world)

3. (Optional) If your students find listening very challenging, do the Additional Support procedure below.

4. Read the instructions: *Listen. These are the eight languages with the most speakers. Where do people speak them? Follow the instructions.*

5. Play Listening Task 1 on the tape. Gesture for students to write the letters on the map.

6. (Optional) To make sure students understand what to do, stop after one or two items. Ask students: *What letter did you write? Where? What language does it stand for?* Then play the rest of Listening Task 1.

7. If necessary, play Listening Task 1 a second time.

8. Check by drawing a rough world map on the board. Have students call out the languages and locations as you write them. (Answers appear in blue on pages 48 and 49.)

ADDITIONAL SUPPORT Have students work in pairs or groups of three. Before they listen, have them look at the map. They write the languages of as many countries as they know. This is to get them thinking about languages and where they are spoken. When they do the activity, if languages they wrote are mentioned, they circle them.

NOTES

• Of course, it is not possible to list every country where a language is used. This is especially true for English, which is used in many countries, often as a "lingua franca" (common language) between people whose native languages are different. An interesting follow-up activity is to have students go on to identify other places, such as Singapore and Zimbabwe, where they know English is used.

• Estimates of language use differ. The information here is based on numbers of native speakers reported in *The Cambridge Encyclopedia of Language* by D. Crystal (Cambridge, 1987).

Culture corner

I. After students have read the Culture Corner, have them answer the question in pairs or small groups: *Does everyone in your country answer the phone the same way?*

2. (Optional) Before students have read the Culture Corner, have them work in groups of three. One student looks at the Culture Corner on page 49. The other two have a single copy of the book between them, opened to the map on pages 68–69. The student looking at page 49 reads the Culture Corner aloud. The others listen. When they hear a country mentioned, they try to be the first to touch it. To do this as a game, the student who touches each country first gets a point.

Note: The reason for having students touch the map is to know who located the country first.

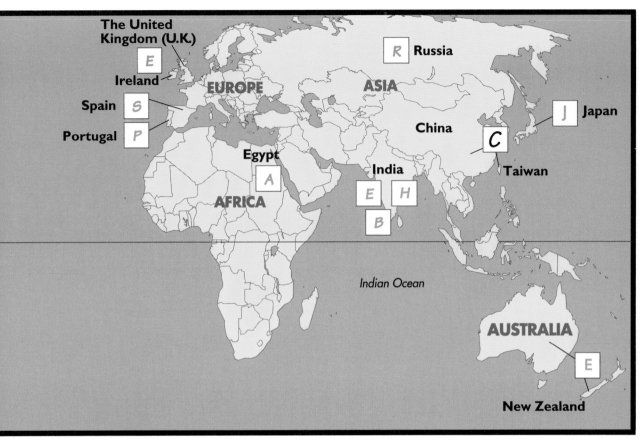

The United Kingdom (U.K.)
E
Ireland
Spain S
Portugal P
EUROPE
Russia R
ASIA
China
Egypt
A
India
AFRICA
E H
B
C
Taiwan
J Japan
Indian Ocean
AUSTRALIA
E
New Zealand

LISTENING TASK 1

World languages

❏ Listen. These are the eight languages with the most speakers.
Where do people speak them? Follow the instructions.

CULTURE CORNER

Even answering the phone can be different from country to country.

• In the U.S., Canada, the U.K., and Australia, people answer with a greeting: *Hello.*
• In Japan, people say *moshi-moshi.* ("Can you hear me?")
• In Korea, people say *yoboseo.* ("Are you there?")
• Some Spanish speakers say *dígame.* It means "tell me."

Does everyone in your country answer the phone the same way?

49

LISTENING TASK 2
Which English?

❏ Look at the words. Can you tell the difference between American and British English?
Write "A" for American.
Write "B" for British.

❏ Now listen to Chris and Helen.
Chris is from the United States.
Helen is from Great Britain.
Correct your answers.

Chris   Helen

1. B lorry
A truck

2. A check
B tick

3. A crib
B cot

4. B aubergine
A eggplant

5. B aluMINium
A aLUminum

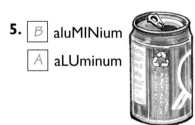

6. A "zee"
B "zed"

YOUR TURN TO TALK

Work in groups of four. What languages do you know words in? What are the words?
What are the languages? Make a list. Which group has the longest list?

Example
A: "Hello" is *hola* in Spanish. French for "thank you" is *merci*.
B: I can say goodbye in Japanese. It's *sayonara*.
C: "One, two, three, four, five" is *um, dois, tres, cuatro, cinco* in Portuguese.

Listening Task 2
Which English?

Listening skill: Distinguishing types of English

1. T: *Look at page 50.*

2. (Optional) Read the title: *"Which English?" What do you think this will be about?* Elicit answers from the students. (Answer: American and British English)

3. (Optional) If your students find listening very challenging, do the Additional Support procedure below.

4. Read the instructions: *Look at the words. Can you tell the difference between American and British English? Write "A" for American. Write "B" for British.*

5. Allow time for students to identify the words and pronunciations they know. If there are some they don't know, they can either guess or leave the boxes blank.

6. Read the second set of instructions: *Now listen to Chris and Helen. Chris is from the United States. Helen is from Great Britain. Correct your answers.*

7. Play Listening Task 1 on the tape. Gesture for students to correct any items they predicted incorrectly.

8. (Optional) Stop the tape at the pause in each item (before the speakers mention which word is American and which is British). Ask students: *Which was American? Which was British?* Then play the answer. This will allow you to check students' answers. (Answers appear in blue on the opposite page.)

9. If necessary, play Listening Task 2 a second time after you have checked, to give students a chance to confirm what they heard.

ADDITIONAL SUPPORT Have students close their books. On one end of the board, write *Chris (USA)*. On the other

end, write *Helen (GB)*. Play Chris's and Helen's self-introductions once or twice so students can hear the difference in accents. Then play the entire tape. The students' task is to identify the accent as quickly as possible. As soon as they know who the speaker is, they point to the name on the board. This activity lets them focus on the accents without worrying about the specific information they'll need when they do the main task.

NOTE

• The purpose of the Additional Support activity is to give students practice in focusing on the speakers' accents. It isn't meant to exaggerate the differences between varieties of English. While minor differences in pronunciation, grammar, and vocabulary exist, they rarely lead to miscommunication.

Your turn to talk

1. Divide the class into groups of four. T: *Work in groups of four. What languages do you know words in? What are the words? What are the languages? Make a list. Which group has the longest list?*

2. (Optional) Demonstrate with the whole class. Encourage a few students to say words they know. If they have trouble getting started, ask: *Who knows how to say "thank you" in another language?*

3. After about five minutes, you may want to have each group put their list on the board.

Optional activity

(For use anytime during or after the unit.)
• ***Words from English.*** Students work in groups of four. They think about their native language(s). In five minutes, they list as many words as possible in their language that are loan words from English. Then they join another group and compare lists. To do the activity as a game, give one point for each word listed.

U N I T   1 6
I like that!

Topic/function: Discussing likes and dislikes
Listening skills: Identifying preferences (Listening Task 1); understanding instructions (Listening Task 2)
Grammar/vocabulary: Infinitives (*to* + verb) and gerunds (verb + *-ing*)

Warming Up

1. Hold your book so that students can see page 51. T: *Look at page 51.*

2. Read the instructions. Pause when you see the symbol ♦ to give students time to answer the questions.

> *Look at the picture. Think about things you like.*
> *Think about things you don't like.*
> *Work with a partner.*
> *Ask each other questions and fill in the chart.*
> *How many things do you agree on?*
> *Write as many things as you can in five minutes.* ♦

3. As students work, circulate and help pairs having difficulty. If any pairs have trouble finding things they agree on, suggest additional topics like sports, TV shows, famous people, etc.

4. Checking answers isn't really necessary. However, it can be interesting to find out which pair listed the most things.

5. (Optional) Have each pair call out their most interesting item. Then have the other students raise their hands to indicate how they feel about the item.

NOTE

• You may want to suggest that students work with someone they don't know very well. This will ensure that they have to discover the information rather than base it on what they already know.

Strategy exercise: *Self-monitoring*

The most successful language learners monitor their own mistakes but also know when they are monitoring too much. Students, individually or collectively, should think about their next step in language learning (the things they need to work on). They should then decide which things are important and which are not.

Optional activity

(For use anytime during or after the unit.)
• *I'd rather be at the beach.* Before class, make a copy of the following worksheet for each student. In class, hand out the worksheets. Students work in groups of three to rank the best five activities for a vacation, then join another group and cut their list to the top three activities. Finally, the combined group decides on the single best vacation activity.

Vacation Worksheet

Which are the best five activities for a vacation?

___ going to the beach
___ seeing a historical place
___ going to a big city
___ going camping
___ going driving
___ playing sports
___ staying home
___ visiting friends or relatives
___ going to a foreign country
___ going to an amusement park

© Cambridge University Press

I like that!

❏ Look at the picture. Think about things you like.
Think about things you don't like.

❏ Work with a partner.
Ask each other questions and fill in the chart.
How many things do you agree on?
Write as many things as you can in five minutes.

SAMPLE
ANSWERS

WE LOVE . . .		WE LIKE . . .	
to travel	___	English	___
ice cream	___	pizza	___
the beach	___	rock music	___
WE DON'T LIKE . . .		**WE HATE . . .**	
carrots	___	math	___
to sing	___	flying	___
snow	___	to study	___

Example
A: Do you like pizza?
B: I love it.
A: I do too.

Same or different?

Sarah

❑ Listen. What things does Sarah like? Check (✔) them.
❑ Do you like the same things? Circle your answers.

1. Places to live    ☐ a house    ✔ an apartment

2. Food    ☐ beef   ☐ fish    ✔ chicken

3. TV   ☐ dramas   ✔ news    ☐ comedies

4. Vacations    ✔ the mountains    ☐ the beach    ☐ a big city

5. School subjects    ☐ English    ☐ math    ✔ history

---

CULTURE CORNER

Many people like to go to other countries on vacation. International travel is popular in most countries. Germans travel the most. In one year recently, three out of every four Germans visited another country. People from the U.S. spend the most money on vacations. Germans are next, and then the Japanese. Where do people from your country go on vacation? Where do you want to go? Is it expensive there?

52

Listening Task 1
Same or different?

Listening skill: Identifying preferences

Note: The tapescript for Unit 16 begins on page T22.

1. T: *Look at page 52.*

2. (Optional) Read the title: *"Same or different?" What do you think this will be about?* Elicit answers from the students. (Answer: comparing their own likes and dislikes to Sarah's)

3. (Optional) If your students find listening very challenging, do the Additional Support procedure below.

4. Read the instructions: *Listen. What things does Sarah like? Check them. Do you like the same things? Circle your answers.*

5. Play Listening Task 1 on the tape. Gesture for students to check Sarah's choices and to circle their own.

6. (Optional) To make sure students understand what to do, stop after the second item. Ask students: *What does Sarah like best – beef, fish, or chicken?* (Answer: chicken) *How about you? Who likes chicken best? Beef? Fish?* Gesture for students to raise their hands. Then play the rest of Listening Task 1.

7. If necessary, play Listening Task 1 a second time.

8. Check by saying the items and having students call out their answers. (Answers appear in blue on the opposite page.)

ADDITIONAL SUPPORT Have students look at the pictures and captions before they listen. They circle their own preferences. Then they listen and check the things Sarah likes. By marking their own choices first, they will be more familiar with the items.

NOTE

• An additional preview activity is to have students look at the items before they listen. They mark the one they think will be the most popular with all the members of the class. Then, or after doing Listening Task 1, read the list. Students raise their hands to show their preferences. Students can see if their predictions were correct.

Culture corner

1. After students have read the Culture Corner, have them answer the questions in pairs or small groups: *Where do people from your country go on vacation? Where do you want to go? Is it expensive there?*

2. (Optional) Before students read the Culture Corner, have them guess the three nationalities that spend the most on vacation. Then they read the Culture Corner to check their predictions.

Optional Activity

(For use anytime during or after the unit.)

• *Forced choices.* Students work in pairs. Write these phrases on the board or dictate them. Students decide which of the two choices they prefer. (If you dictate, they write only the one of each pair they prefer.) They have to give at least two reasons for each choice.

1. a vacation in Paris or Cairo
2. a vacation in Hawaii or Alaska
3. staying in a luxury hotel or staying with relatives

Now try more difficult choices:

4. having an exotic but dangerous vacation or a comfortable but boring one
5. flying in an airplane during a storm or riding in a bus on an icy road
6. getting sick in a foreign country or losing all your money

Listening Task 2
How about you?

Listening skill: Understanding instructions

I. T: *Look at page 53.*

2. (Optional) Read the title: *"How about you?" What do you think this will be about?* Elicit answers from the students. (Answer: students' own preferences)

3. (Optional) If your students find listening very challenging, do the Additional Support procedure below.

4. Read the instructions: *Listen. What do you like to do? What don't you like to do? Answer the questions with your own ideas.*

5. Play Listening Task 2 on the tape. Gesture for students to complete the sentences.

6. (Optional) To make sure students understand what to do, stop after the first item. Ask students: *What did you write in the purple circle? What did you write in the green circle?* Encourage several students to answer. Then play the rest of Listening Task 2.

7. If necessary, play Listening Task 2 a second time. Before replaying the tape, you may want to have students compare answers to make sure they understood the topic for each shape.

8. Check answers by saying the name and color of each shape. Encourage a few students to say what they wrote. Restate the topic for the item: *The purple circle is something you love to eat.*

ADDITIONAL SUPPORT Write the following words on the board: *circle, diamond, square, triangle.* Play the tape once. Students listen for these words. They raise their hands or make a mark on a piece of paper each time they hear one.

NOTES

• This lesson uses gerunds and infinitives. Gerunds are *-ing* forms of verbs, which are used as nouns. Infinitives are verbs usually used with *to.* Some verbs can be used with either a gerund or an infinitive. (Example: I love swimming. I love to swim.) *Like* and *hate* are also in this group. Other verbs can be used only with gerunds. (Example: I enjoy swimming.) *Dislike* also takes only the gerund. Other verbs can take only the infinitive. (Example: I want to go there.) *Want* and *hope* are common examples.

• You may prefer to check answers after each segment rather than waiting until students have heard all four items.

Your turn to talk

I. Divide the class into pairs. T: *Work with a partner. Look at your partner's sentences on this page. Ask about them. When your partner asks about your sentences, say at least three things about each.*

2. (Optional) Demonstrate the activity: Write an interesting answer about yourself on the board. Encourage students to ask you questions. Answer with at least three sentences. As you do, count the sentences on your fingers or on the board to emphasize that saying at least three sentences is part of the task.

3. (Optional) (after about 10 minutes) T: *What was your partner's most interesting answer?* Encourage several students to respond.

LISTENING **TASK 2**

How about you?

❏ Listen. What do you like to do? What don't you like to do?
Answer the questions with your own ideas.

SAMPLE ANSWERS

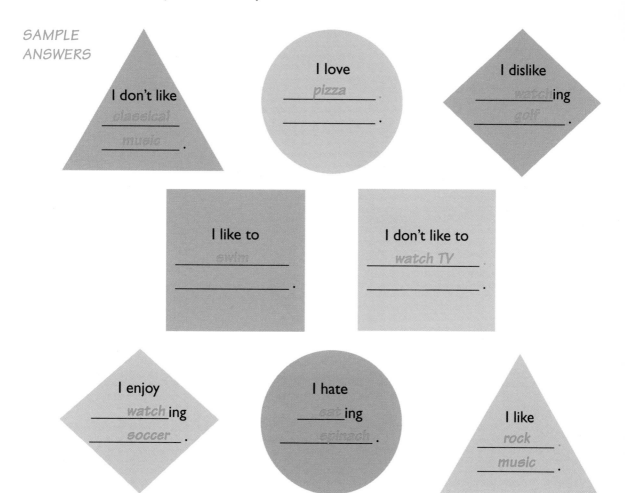

I don't like
classical
music .

I love
pizza .
_____ .

I dislike
*watch*ing
golf .

I like to
swim
_____ .

I don't like to
watch TV .
_____ .

I enjoy
*watch*ing
soccer .

I hate
*eat*ing
spinach .

I like
rock
music .

YOUR TURN TO TALK

Work with a partner. Look at your partner's sentences on this page. Ask about them. When your partner asks about your sentences, say at least three things about each.

Example
A: So, you love fish.
B: Yes, I eat it about three times a week.
My favorite kind is tuna.
I like it grilled.

Strange news

WARMING UP

❑ Work with a partner.
These pictures are from an unusual newspaper.
Which words do you think go with each picture?
Write them in the boxes. Some boxes have two words.

~~earth~~   kangaroos   soccer   ~~UFO~~
elephant   loses   statue

❑ What do you want to know about each picture?
Write one question for each.

SAMPLE
ANSWERS

| earth, UFO |

1. _Where is it from?_

| kangaroos |

2. _Where are they?_

| statue |

3. _Who is this?_

| loses |

4. _How did he lose_
   weight?

| elephant, soccer |

5. _Can the elephant_
   play soccer?

54

UNIT 17
Strange news

Topic/function: Evaluating newspaper
headlines and stories
Listening skills: Understanding newspaper
headlines (Listening Task 1);
understanding summaries, evaluating
information (Listening Task 2)
Grammar/vocabulary: Simple past

Warming Up

1. Hold your book so that students can see
page 54. T: *Look at page 54.*

2. Read the instructions. Pause when you
see the symbol ♦ to give students time to
answer the questions.

> *Work with a partner.*
> *These pictures are from an unusual
>   newspaper.*
> *Which words do you think go with each
>   picture?*
> *Write them in the boxes. Some boxes have two
>   words.* ♦

3. As students work, circulate and help
pairs having difficulty. If there are words
students don't know, encourage them to
skip those for the moment. If they do the
ones they know first, some of the words
may become easier to guess.

4. After a few minutes, read the second set
of instructions:

> *What do you want to know about each
>   picture?*
> *Write one question for each.* ♦

5. Give students time to work. Circulate
and help pairs having difficulty.

6. Check answers by having students call
out the words they wrote for each picture.
It isn't necessary to have more than a few
students volunteer their questions.

NOTE

• These stories are based on stories that
appeared in *Weekly World News* and the

National Examiner. Both are popular, often
selling more than a million copies a week
each. These are sometimes referred to as
"supermarket newspapers" because that's
where they are usually sold. They are often
placed next to the cash register where the
papers' surprising headlines catch shoppers'
attention as they wait in line. Most people
do not take the papers very seriously.

Strategy exercise: *Linking learning to the world*

This unit gives students another
opportunity to think about how much they
know about the world outside the
classroom and how they use that
knowledge in the classroom. Students can
prepare a "typical" newscast for the week,
or they might want to continue with the
"strange news" theme of the unit.

Optional activity

(For use anytime during or after the unit.)

• **The real papers.** Get a few copies of real
issues of newspapers that feature stories
such as these. You'll need one newspaper
story for each student. Distribute the
stories. Students read the stories and
prepare a short oral summary of the story.
They then find a partner and deliver the
summary. Partners should ask at least one
question. You may want students to
continue until they've talked to three or
four different partners.

A follow-up activity that helps develop
critical reading and thinking skills is to
have students look for proof that the story
isn't true. To do this, they should think
about the kind of information they expect
to find in a newspaper story. Often, this is
information related to *Wh-* questions:
What happened? Who did it happen to?
Where did it happen? When did it
happen? Very often, these stories are
missing important information such as
dates, places, company names, etc.

Listening Task 1
What . . . ?!

> **Listening skill:** Understanding newspaper headlines

Note: The tapescript for Unit 17 begins on page T23.

1. T: *Look at page 55.*

2. (Optional) Read the title: *"What . . . ?!"* *What do you think this will be about?* Elicit answers from the students. (Answer: the stories that go with the pictures in Warming Up)

3. (Optional) If your students find listening very challenging, do the Additional Support procedure below.

4. Read the instructions: *Listen. What are these stories about? Write the newspaper headlines.*

5. Play Listening Task 1 on the tape. Gesture for students to write their answers.

6. (Optional) To make sure students understand what to do, stop after the second item. Ask students: *What's the headline for number two?* (Answer: GIANT KANGAROOS ATTACK SCHOOL) Then play the rest of Listening Task 1.

7. If necessary, play Listening Task 1 a second time.

8. Check by having students call out their answers. You may want to write them on the board. (Answers appear in blue on the opposite page.)

ADDITIONAL SUPPORT Students work in pairs. Before they listen, they look at the pictures on page 54 and try to match them to the news stories on this page. Then they guess what the missing words in the headlines will be.

NOTES

- Stories of UFOs and drastic weight loss are a very common feature of supermarket newspapers.
- Interestingly, both *Weekly World News* and the *National Examiner* carried stories about the statue of the rock and roll singer. The stories, which were published about two years apart, both carried photographs of a similar statue. One paper said it was from Egypt and the other from Greece. Both papers said it was evidence that singer Elvis Presley had been reincarnated (had lived before as someone else).

Culture corner

1. After students have read the Culture Corner, have them answer the questions in pairs or small groups: *Are there newspapers with strange stories in your country? What kinds of stories? Do you believe them?*

2. (Optional) After students have read the Culture Corner, have them do this activity to make them more aware of syllable stress. Have them look through the Culture Corner and underline all the words with three or more syllables. Elicit the words, and write them on the board. The list should be as follows (don't indicate the stressed syllable when you write):

1. **Uni**ted
2. **Can**ada
3. un**usu**al
4. **news**papers
5. **pop**ular
6. **vis**itors
7. **an**imals
8. **med**ical
9. es**pe**cially

Say each word. Have students repeat the words. As they repeat, they quickly stand up on the accented syllable. (Stressed syllables are in bold, above.)

We learned this activity from Yoko Narahashi.

LISTENING **TASK 1**

What . . . ?!

❑ Listen. What are these stories about?
Write the newspaper headlines.

1.

UFO SENDS TV SPORTS SHOW TO EARTH

Lorem ipsum dolor sit amet, consectetuer adipiscing elit, sed diam nonummy nibh euismod tincidunt ut laoreet dolore magna aliquam erat volutpat. Ut wisi enim ad minim veniam, quis nostrud exerci tation ullamcorper suscipit lobortis nisl ut aliquip ex ea commodo consequat. Duis autem vel eum iriure dolor in hendrerit in vulputate velit esse molestie consequat, vel illum dolore eu feugiat nulla facilisis at vero eros et accumsan et iusto odio dignissim qui blandit praesent luptatum zzril delenit augue duis dolore te feugait nulla facilisi.

Lorem ipsum dolor sit amet, consectetuer adipiscing elit, sed diam nonummy nibh euismod tincidunt ut laoreet dolore magna aliquam erat volutpat. Ut wisi enim ad minim veniam, quis nostrud exerci tation ullamcorper suscipit lobortis nisl ut aliquip ex ea commodo consequat. Duis autem vel eum iriure dolor in

2.

GIANT ~~KANGAROOS~~ ATTACK ~~SCHOOL~~

Lorem ipsum dolor sit amet, consectetuer adipiscing elit, sed diam nonummy nibh euismod tincidunt ut laoreet dolore magna aliquam erat volutpat. Ut wisi enim ad minim veniam, quis nostrud exerci tation ullamcorper suscipit lobortis nisl ut aliquip ex ea commodo consequat. Duis autem vel eum iriure dolor in hendrerit in vulputate velit esse molestie consequat, vel illum dolore eu feugiat nulla facilisis at vero eros et accumsan et iusto odio dignissim qui blandit praesent luptatum zzril delenit augue duis dolore te feugait nulla facilisi. Nam liber tempor cum soluta nobis eleifend option congue nihil imperdiet doming id quod mazim placerat facer possim assum. Lorem ipsum dolor sit amet, consectetuer adipiscing elit, sed diam nonummy nibh euismod tincidunt ut laoreet dolore magna

3.

2,000-YEAR-OLD GREEK ~~STATUE~~ HAS FACE OF ~~ROCK~~ ~~STAR~~

Lorem ipsum dolor sit amet, consectetuer adipiscing elit, sed diam nonummy nibh euismod tincidunt ut laoreet dolore magna aliquam erat volutpat. Ut wisi enim ad minim veniam, quis nostrud exerci tation ullamcorper suscipit lobortis nisl ut aliquip ex ea commodo consequat. Duis autem vel eum iriure dolor in hendrerit in vulputate velit esse molestie consequat, vel illum dolore eu feugiat nulla facilisis at vero eros et accumsan et iusto odio dignissim qui blandit praesent luptatum zzril delenit augue duis dolore te feugait nulla facilisi. Lorem ipsum dolor sit amet, consectetuer adipiscing elit, sed diam nonummy nibh euismod tincidunt ut laoreet dolore magna aliquam erat volutpat. Ut wisi enim ad minim veniam, quis nostrud exerci tation ullamcorper suscipit lobortis nisl ut aliquip ex ea commodo consequat.

Lorem ipsum dolor sit amet, consectetuer adipiscing elit, sed diam nonummy nibh euismod tincidunt ut laoreet dolore magna aliquam erat volutpat. Ut wisi enim ad minim veniam, quis nostrud exerci tation ullamcorper suscipit lobortis nisl ut aliquip ex ea commodo consequat. Duis autem vel eum iriure dolor in hendrerit in vulputate velit esse molestie consequat, vel illum dolore eu feugiat nulla facilisis at vero eros et accumsan et iusto odio dignissim qui blandit praesent luptatum zzril delenit augue duis dolore te feugait

4.

~~MAN~~ ~~LOSES~~
100 POUNDS

Lorem ipsum dolor sit amet, consectetuer adipiscing elit, sed diam nonummy nibh euismod tincidunt ut laoreet dolore magna aliquam erat volutpat. Ut wisi enim ad minim veniam, quis nostrud exerci tation ullamcorper suscipit lobortis nisl ut aliquip ex ea commodo consequat. Lorem ipsum dolor sit amet, consectetuer adipiscing elit, sed diam nonummy nibh euismod tincidunt ut laoreet dolore magna aliquam erat volutpat. Ut wisi enim ad minim veniam, quis nostrud exerci tation ullamcorper suscipit lobortis nisl ut aliquip ex ea commodo consequat. Duis autem vel eum iriure dolor in hendrerit in vulputate velit esse molestie consequat, vel illum dolore eu feugiat nulla facilisis at vero eros et accumsan et iusto odio dignissim qui blandit praesent luptatum zzril delenit augue. Lorem ipsum dolor sit amet, consectetuer adipiscing elit, sed diam nonummy nibh euismod tincidunt ut laoreet dolore magna aliquam erat volutpat. Ut wisi

5.

~~ELEPHANT~~ JOINS
~~SOCCER~~ ~~TEAM~~

Lorem ipsum dolor sit amet, consectetuer adipiscing elit, sed diam nonummy nibh euismod tincidunt ut laoreet dolore magna aliquam erat volutpat. Ut wisi enim ad minim veniam, quis nostrud exerci tation ullamcorper suscipit lobortis nisl ut aliquip ex ea commodo consequat. Duis autem vel eum iriure dolor in hendrerit in vulputate velit esse molestie consequat, vel illum dolore eu feugiat nulla facilisis at vero eros et accumsan et iusto odio dignissim qui blandit praesent luptatum zzril delenit augue duis dolore te feugait nulla facilisi.

Lorem ipsum dolor sit amet, consectetuer adipiscing elit, sed diam nonummy nibh euismod tincidunt ut laoreet dolore magna aliquam erat volutpat. Ut wisi enim ad minim veniam, quis nostrud exerci tation ullamcorper suscipit lobortis nisl ut aliquip ex ea commodo consequat. Duis autem vel eum iriure dolor in hendrerit in vulputate velit esse molestie consequat, vel illum dolore eu feugiat nulla facilisis at vero eros et accumsan et iusto

CULTURE CORNER

In the United States and Canada, several unusual newspapers report strange stories. Many people say they are not always true. These are some of the most popular topics:

- stories about famous people
- UFOs and visitors from space
- strange things about animals
- new diets (ways to lose weight)
- health and medical news
- old rock stars, especially Elvis Presley

Are there newspapers with strange stories in your country? What kinds of stories? Do you believe them?

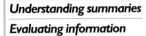

LISTENING TASK **2** *Do you believe it?*

❏ Listen to these stories.
What information is in the stories? Check (✔) your answers.

❏ Do you think these stories might be true?
Draw lines to show your opinion.

True?

Maybe Probably not Impossible

1. UFO sends TV sports show to earth.
   ☐ Videotape of UFO sports show found on earth.
   ☑ People on earth saw a TV show from a UFO.
   The show was about sports.

2. Giant kangaroos attack school.
   ☐ The school was damaged, and many students
   were hurt.
   ☑ The school was damaged, but no students
   were hurt.

3. Two-thousand-year-old Greek statue has face of
   rock star.
   ☑ The statue looks like a rock star.
   ☐ The rock star was Greek.

4. Man loses 100 pounds.
   ☐ He stopped eating.
   ☑ He only ate one kind of food.

5. Elephant joins soccer team.
   ☑ The elephant does tricks before soccer games.
   ☐ The elephant is a good soccer player.

YOUR TURN TO TALK

Work in pairs. Think of a very unusual story. Answer these questions:

• What happened?   • When did it happen?
• Who did it happen to?   • Where did it happen?

Now change partners. Ask your partner questions about his or her story. Then answer your partner's questions about your story.

Listening Task 2
Do you believe it?

Listening skills: Understanding summaries, evaluating information

1. T: *Look at page 56.*

2. (Optional) Read the title: *"Do you believe it?"* What do you think this will be about? Elicit answers from the students. (Answer: whether or not students think these stories are possible)

3. Read the instructions: *Listen to these stories. What information is in the stories? Check your answers. Do you think these stories might be true? Draw lines to show your opinion.*

4. Play Listening Task 2 on the tape. Gesture for students to check the story summaries and to draw lines.

5. (Optional) If your students find listening very challenging, do the Additional Support procedure below.

6. (Optional) To make sure students understand what to do, stop after the second item. Ask students: *What is the story about?* (Answer: The school was damaged, but no students were hurt.) *Is the story true? Maybe? Probably not? Impossible?* Gesture for them to raise their hands to show what they think. Then play the rest of Listening Task 2.

7. If necessary, play Listening Task 2 a second time.

8. Check answers by reading the headlines. Have students call out the summaries they checked. Have them raise their hands to show whether or not they believe the stories. (Answers appear in blue on the opposite page.)

ADDITIONAL SUPPORT Have students work in pairs. Stop after each item. Have them talk about what they heard. They should try to agree on the summaries. Their opinions may be different.

NOTE
• It is clear that these stories are not very serious. They are included in this book because the unusual content makes them interesting and amusing to students.

Your turn to talk

1. Divide the class into pairs. T: *Work in pairs. Think of a very unusual story. Answer these questions: What happened? Who did it happen to? When did it happen? Where did it happen?*

2. As students work, circulate and help those having difficulty. If pairs are having trouble thinking of a story, have them look at the topics in the Culture Corner on page 55. The more specific their ideas, the easier it is to think of the story. For example, if they choose a famous person, they should decide who.

3. (after about five minutes) T: *Now change partners. Ask your partner questions about his or her story. Then answer your partner's questions about your story.*

4. (Optional) As a full class or in larger groups of ten or twelve, have students summarize their partner's stories. The group then decides which story was the most unusual.

Optional activities

(For use anytime during or after the unit.)
• ***Your teacher has been kidnapped!*** Tell students that you were kidnapped by a UFO. Have them work in pairs to make up a suitable story.

• ***What's the story?*** Once students understand the spirit of the stories in this unit (outrageous!), they work in pairs. They think of the most outrageous story possible. Then they write a headline for their story. Each pair joins another pair. The new partners look at the headline and ask as many questions as possible in five minutes.

U N I T   1 8
Holidays

Topic/function: Talking about holidays and customs in different countries
Listening skills: Identifying dates (Listening Task 1); identifying events (Listening Task 2)
Grammar/vocabulary: Present tenses: present of *be* and simple present for descriptions

Warming Up

1. Hold your book so that students can see page 57. T: *Look at page 57.*

2. Read the instructions. Pause when you see the symbol ♦ to give students time to answer the questions.

> *Work with a partner.*
> *Think about holidays in your country or other countries.*
> *When do people do the things in the pictures?*
> *Write the name of a holiday for as many pictures as you can.* ♦

3. As students work, circulate and help pairs having difficulty.

4. (after a few minutes) T: *How many other holidays can you list?*

5. Check answers by saying the name of each picture. Students call out the names of holidays.

NOTES

• The pictures are meant only to make the vocabulary clear. Holidays in the students' country or countries may include very different styles of the same items.

• Some holiday names, such as New Year's, are usually translated into English. Others, such as Islam's Ramadan and Japan's Obon, are not. There are no consistent rules that tell when and when

not to translate. Encourage students to try to say the holidays in English. It can be good practice in explaining one's own culture in English.

Strategy exercise: *Semantic mapping*

Semantic mapping is a technique that helps students think about the words they are likely to hear in a given passage. It also helps students associate new words with old words. One way to help students to practice this strategy is to draw several circles with spokes coming out of them on the board. Choose a holiday and write it in the circle. Students work in pairs to write the things associated with the holiday on the spokes. Set a three to five minute time limit. Pairs see how many words related to the topic they can list in the given time.

Optional activities

(For use anytime during or after the unit.)

• *Mouth marathon.* Students work in pairs. Assign the topic "Holiday memories." If they have already done Your Turn to Talk, tell them to use a different holiday from the one they used there. Individually, students speak for as long as they can about a specific holiday memory. The other student in the pair listens. Whenever the speaker pauses, the listener counts the length of time in his/her head or behind his/her back. If the speaker stops talking for longer than three seconds, the next speaker begins. The speaker may keep the floor by using fillers like, "Um," "Er," "What I mean to say is . . . ." The one who speaks the longest wins. This is based on an activity developed by L. A. Meagher.

• *Story time.* Tell the story of the origins of a holiday (if possible, illustrating with pictures). After listening, the students reconstruct the story in pairs.

Holidays

☐ Work with a partner.
Think about holidays in your country or other countries.
When do people do the things in the pictures?
Write the name of a holiday for as many pictures as
you can.

SAMPLE
ANSWERS

go dancing
Carnival

have fireworks
Fourth of July

ring bells
New Year's Eve

light candles
Chanukah

eat special food
Thanksgiving

visit relatives
Christmas

eat candy

Halloween

go to a parade

Labor Day

remember someone
who has died

Obon

☐ How many other holidays can you list?

Ramadan _____   _____

Cinco de Mayo _____   _____

_____   _____

Fireworks, food, and fun

❏ Listen. People are talking about these holidays.
When are they?
Write the numbers on the correct months. One item has two answers.

1. Martin Luther King Day (U.S.)
2. Moon Festival (China)
3. St. Patrick's Day (Ireland, U.S.)
4. Thanksgiving (U.S.)
5. Thanksgiving (Canada)

6. The Day of the Dead (Mexico)
7. St. Lucia's Day (Sweden)
8. Independence Day (U.S.)
9. Children's Day (Japan)

January	**April**	**July**	**October**
1		8	2, 5
February	**May**	**August**	**November**
	9		4, 6
March	**June**	**September**	**December**
3		2	7

CULTURE CORNER

In some countries, people make promises on New Year's Day. They say they will change or do something different in the new year. These promises are called "resolutions." Here are the most popular resolutions in the United States:

- Lose weight
- Make or save money
- Stop smoking
- Change something about your job or get a better job
- Exercise more

Do people really change? Some do, but most only keep their resolutions about one month. Less than 20 percent keep them more than two years. Do you celebrate the new year? Do you make "New Year's resolutions"?

Listening Task 1
Fireworks, food, and fun

Listening skill: Identifying dates

Note: The tapescript for Unit 18 begins on page T24.

1. T: *Look at page 58.*

2. (Optional) Read the title: *"Fireworks, food, and fun." What do you think this will be about?* Elicit answers from the students. (Answer: things people do during holidays)

3. Read the instructions: *Listen. People are talking about these holidays. When are they? Write the numbers on the correct months. One item has two answers.*

4. Play Listening Task 1 on the tape. Gesture for students to write the numbers on the calendar.

5. (Optional) If your students find listening very challenging, do the Additional Support procedure below.

6. If necessary, play Listening Task 1 a second time.

7. Check answers by saying the names of the holidays and having students call out the months. (Answers appear in blue on the opposite page.)

ADDITIONAL SUPPORT Have students do Listening Task 1 in pairs. Stop after each item and give time for them to talk about what they understood before they answer.

NOTE

• Students often confuse the terms "holiday," "festival," "vacation," and "day off." The usual meanings are as follows:

Holidays are special days that celebrate something such as a religious or historical event, a person, or an idea. On official holidays such as New Year's (in most countries), most people do not go to work or school. On unofficial holidays, such as Valentine's Day and Halloween in the U.S., people have to go to work or school.

Festivals are similar to holidays but often involve public gatherings. Also, they often last more than one day.

Vacations are days off from work planned by individuals.

Culture corner

1. After students have read the Culture Corner, have them answer the questions in pairs or small groups: *Do you celebrate the new year? Do you make "New Year's resolutions"?*

2. (Optional) Before class, make copies of the Culture Corner. You'll need one copy for every two students. On the copies, delete the key words in each resolution: 1. weight, 2. money 3. smoking, 4. job (both times), 5. exercise. Divide the students into pairs. They read the copies and guess the missing words. Then they check their book to see if they were correct.

Optional activities

(For use anytime during or after the unit.)
• *Parts of a holiday.* Students work in small groups. They first choose a holiday, then write all the nouns, verbs, and adjectives (usually feelings) associated with the holiday. OR Assign a holiday to the whole class and have the groups compete against each other to see how many words they can write in a given time.

• *You really should.* As a variation on the above activity, students work in groups but write down the following for a certain holiday:
   1. things one has to do
   2. things one should do
   3. things one should never do.

Listening Task 2
Good times

Listening skill: Identifying events

1. T: *Look at page 59.*

2. (Optional) Read the title: *"Good times."* *What do you think this will be about?* Elicit answers from the students. (Answer: holidays in different countries)

3. (Optional) If your students find listening very challenging, do the Additional Support procedure below.

4. Read the instructions: *Listen. You will hear about holidays around the world. Number the pictures, one through four. Write one more thing about each holiday.*

5. Play Listening Task 2 on the tape. Gesture for students to number the pictures and write (at least) one more thing about each holiday.

6. (Optional) To make sure students understand what to do, stop after the first item. Ask students: *Which picture?* (Answer: kite flying) *What else did you write?* Encourage several students to answer. Then play the rest of Listening Task 2.

7. If necessary, play Listening Task 2 a second time. Before replaying the tape, you may want to have students compare their answers in pairs: *Work with a partner. Look at your partner's answers. How many were the same? Then we'll listen again.*

8. Check answers. Ask: *What's number 2? What did you write about it?* (etc.) (Answers appear in blue on the opposite page.)

ADDITIONAL SUPPORT Have students work in groups of two or three. They look at the pictures and write two or three words for each, describing objects or people's actions. Then, when they do the Listening Task itself, play the tape twice.

The first time, they only try to number the pictures. The second time they try to catch extra information.

Your turn to talk

1. T: *Choose a holiday you remember very well. Who were you with? Where were you? What made the day special?*

2. (Optional) To help students clearly remember the holiday, have them close their eyes. Slowly ask a series of *Wh-* questions to help them remember. (Examples: What did you do? What was the weather like?) This can help prepare them for the task that follows.

3. Divide the class into pairs. T: *Work with a partner. Talk about the holiday for 90 seconds.* Gesture for one student (A) in each pair to begin.

4. (after 90 seconds) T: *Stop. Now listen to your partner for 90 seconds.* Gesture for the B's to begin.

5. (after 90 seconds) T: *Stop. A's, stand up. Find a new partner.*

6. Continue by repeating Steps 3–5 two more times. The new time limits are 60 seconds and 45 seconds, respectively.

NOTES

• Make sure the students understand that their speaking is not conversation. It is more like giving "mini-speeches."

• If time allows, have the listeners ask two or three questions after each "mini-speech." The questions can help the speakers know what wasn't clear.

• This activity is based on "Fluency Workshop" by Keith Maurice. Since students tell essentially the same story three times, it becomes easier. Some students report that by the third round, they don't have to "think about English/how to say things." In many cases, they are thinking in English and, thus, aren't thinking about how to say things.

Good times

❏ Listen. You will hear about holidays around the world.
Number the pictures (1–4).
Write one more thing about each holiday.

| 2 | Water Festival

people throw water

| 3 | Carnival

parades, dancing

| 4 | Chinese New Year

lasts four days

| I | Kite flying

"No bad luck" on kites

YOUR
TURN TO
TALK

Choose a holiday you remember very well. Who were you with? Where were you?
What made the day special?

• Work with a partner. Talk about the holiday for 90 seconds. Then listen to your
partner for 90 seconds.

• Now change partners. This time, talk for 60 seconds. Listen to your partner.

• Change partners again. This time, talk for 45 seconds. Then listen to your new
partner. Can you say the same things in only 45 seconds?

59

Inventions

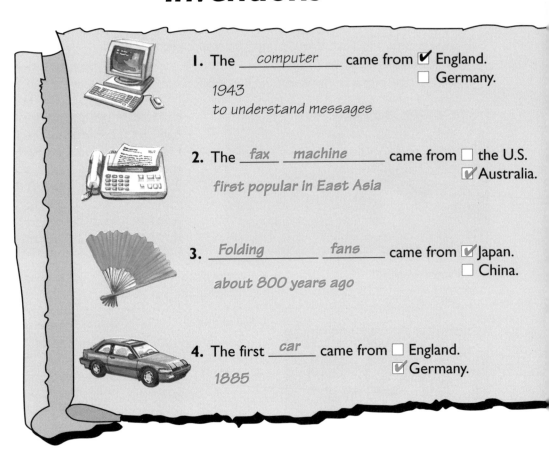

1. The _____computer_____ came from ☑ England.
   ☐ Germany.
   1943
   to understand messages

2. The __fax__ __machine__ came from ☐ the U.S.
   ☑ Australia.
   first popular in East Asia

3. __Folding__ __fans__ came from ☑ Japan.
   ☐ China.
   about 800 years ago

4. The first __car__ came from ☐ England.
   ☑ Germany.
   1885

WARMING UP

❏ Look at the pictures on pages 60–61.
Match these words to the correct pictures.
Write the words on the lines above.

calendar   clock   folding fans
car   ~~computer~~   puppets
chocolate bar   fax machine

❏ Work with a partner.
Where do you think these things came from?
Check (✔) the places.

Inventions

Topic/function: Describing inventions and where they came from

Listening skills: Understanding specific information (Listening Task 1); identifying the purpose of something (Listening Task 2)

Grammar/vocabulary: Infinitive of purpose: *You can use it to . . .*

Warming Up

1. Hold your book so that students can see page 60. T: *Look at page 60.*

2. Read the instructions. Pause when you see the symbol ♦ to give students time to answer the questions.

> *Look at the pictures on pages 60 to 61.*
> *Match these words to the correct pictures.*
> *Write the words on the lines above.* ♦

3. As students work, circulate and help those having difficulty.

4. Check answers by saying the numbers and having students say the words. T: *Number 1 is a computer. What's number 2?* (Answer: a fax machine), etc.

5. Read the rest of the instructions:

> *Work with a partner.*
> *Where do you think these things came from?*
> *Check the places.* ♦

6. As students work, circulate and help pairs having difficulty.

7. There is no need to check answers as students will get them in Listening Task 1.

NOTE

• Make sure the students understand that this is a game. There is no reason that they "should" know the answers.

Strategy exercise: New words in context

Students often rely on their dictionaries too much. Dictionaries are useful, but like any tool, they need to be used correctly.

Students should not look up every new word they see or hear. One way to help them guess meaning is to give them a series of sentences using a new word. Each sentence gives a clue about the meaning. Students guess, usually in their native languages, the meaning of the word. For example, students may not know the word "puppet." Try reading the following clues for "puppet" and have the students guess the meaning:

1. A puppet is a kind of doll.
2. A puppet is often worn on the hand.
3. People "speak" for the puppet.

Repeat the procedure with other unfamiliar words.

Optional activity

(For use anytime during or after the unit.)

• **"100 years ago" chalkboard race.** Have students work in as many groups as you have space for at the chalkboard. The groups stand in lines in front of their section of the board. The first person in each line has a piece of chalk. You announce the topic, then say "Go." The person with the chalk runs to the board and writes one item that matches the topic. (Example: Things in the kitchen – refrigerator) That person runs back to his or her line and gives the chalk to the second person. The second person runs to the board and writes another item. Then continue. Allow about one minute for each topic.

> **Topics:**
> 100 years ago we did not have . . .
>> these things in the kitchen
>> these machines that make life easier
>> these things made of plastic
>> these things that students have
>> these sounds
>> these terrible things
>> these wonderful things

Listening Task 1
Where in the world?

Listening skill: Understanding specific information

Note: The tapescript for Unit 19 begins on page T26.

1. T: *Look at page 61. Now we'll find out the answers.*

2. Read the instructions: *Listen. Were your guesses right? Correct your answers. Write one more fact about each invention.*

3. Play Listening Task 1 on the tape. Gesture for students to correct any mistakes they made when they guessed. They should also write one more thing about each item.

4. (Optional) If your students find listening very challenging, do the Additional Support procedure below.

5. (Optional) To make sure students understand what to do, stop after the second item. Ask students: *Where was the fax machine invented?* (Answer: Australia) *What else did you write?* (Possible answer: first popular in East Asia because of the writing system) Then play the rest of Listening Task 1.

6. If necessary, play Listening Task 1 again. Before replaying the tape, you may want to have students work in pairs to compare the extra information they wrote: *Work with a partner. Look at your partner's extra information. Did you write the same thing? Then we'll listen again.*

7. Check by saying the names of the inventions. Students should call out the countries and the extra information. (Answers appear in blue on pages 60 and 61.)

ADDITIONAL SUPPORT Do Listening Task 1 in two parts. The first time, the students are listening only to find out the country where each thing was invented. The second time, they try to catch an extra fact. You may want to have them do the second part in pairs. Pause after each item to let them talk about what they understood.

NOTES

• You may want to stop the tape before each item and poll the students as to which country they think each invention is from. You may want to do the activity as a game, giving students one point for each correct guess.

• The information in this activity came from a variety of sources including *The Guinness Book of World Records,* D. McFarlan, editor (Guinness Publishing) and *The Dictionary of Misinformation* by T. Burnham (Harper & Row), a delightful book which, despite its title, aims at correcting misinformation rather than spreading it.

Culture corner

1. After students have read the Culture Corner, have them answer the question in pairs or small groups: *What inventions come from your country?*

2. (Optional) Before students have read the Culture Corner, have them look at the map on pages 68–69. Dictate the following inventions: *printing press, light bulb.* Students write them on the place they think each was invented. They then read the Culture Corner and draw lines from the words they wrote to the places where they really originated.

Optional Activity

(For use anytime during or after the unit.)

• *That's a crazy idea.* Have students work in small groups to design a strange (and perhaps useless) invention such as those in Listening Task 2. They should draw a picture. After they finish, have them tell a larger group or the whole class about their invention.

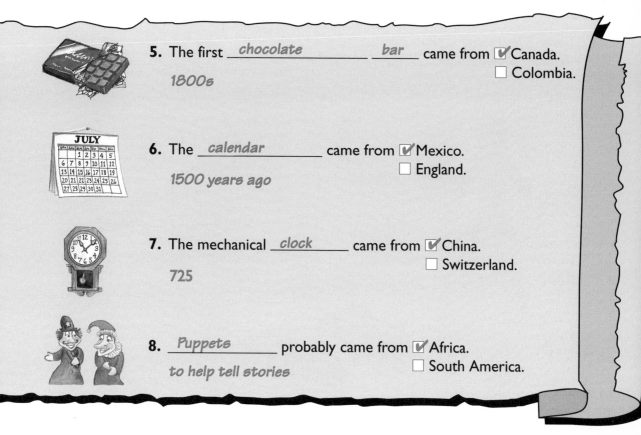

5. The first _chocolate_ _bar_ came from ☑ Canada.
☐ Colombia.

1800s

6. The _calendar_ came from ☑ Mexico.
☐ England.

1500 years ago

7. The mechanical _clock_ came from ☑ China.
☐ Switzerland.

725

8. _Puppets_ probably came from ☑ Africa.
☐ South America.

to help tell stories

LISTENING TASK 1

Where in the world?

❏ Listen. Were your guesses right?
Correct your answers.
Write one more fact about each invention.

CULTURE CORNER

Many inventions don't come from the places that most people think they do. For example, the first printing press with letters that move wasn't from Germany. It came from Korea in 1234. That's 200 years before the first press in Europe. Most people think the light bulb came from the United States, but Thomas Edison didn't invent it. He just made it better. Sir Joseph William Swan made the first real light bulb in England in 1860. What inventions come from your country?

That's really strange!

❑ Listen. These are real products.
What are they used for? Write your answers.

❑ Would you want these items? Which ones? Circle them.

1. These will help keep __insects__ off you.

2. She bought this to eat __spaghetti__ .

3. With these mops, your __cat__ can __clean__ the floor.

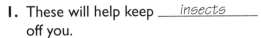

4. She made this to __sit__ __down__ on the train.

5. He uses it to __open__ __letters__ .

YOUR TURN TO TALK

Work in pairs. Imagine you're inventors. You're making a machine. The machine will do something you don't like to do. What will your machine do? What will it look like? Now join another pair. Tell your new partners about your machine.

Example: Our machine is a _____ . We use it to _____ . . . .

Listening Task 2
That's really strange!

> **Listening skill:** Identifying the purpose of something

1. T: *Look at page 62.*

2. (Optional) Read the title: *"That's really strange!" What do you think this will be about?* Elicit answers from the students. (Answer: unusual inventions)

3. (Optional) If your students find listening very challenging, do the Additional Support procedure below.

4. Read the instructions: *Listen. These are real products. What are they used for? Write your answers. Would you want these items? Which ones? Circle them.*

5. Play Listening Task 2 on the tape. Gesture for students to write the uses and to circle the items they would want.

6. (Optional) To make sure students understand what to do, stop after the second item. T: *She bought this to eat spaghetti. Would you want one? Who circled this?* Gesture for students to raise their hands to show their answers. Then play the rest of Listening Task 2.

7. If necessary, play Listening Task 2 a second time.

8. Check answers by saying the sentences and having students complete them. Have students raise their hands to show whether or not they'd want the item. (Answers appear in blue on the opposite page.)

ADDITIONAL SUPPORT Have students work in pairs. They look at each invention and guess what each item is used for, writing the information on the line. As a way of helping them visualize the inventions, you may want students to guess the size of each item and the material it is made from.

NOTES

• You may prefer to check answers after each segment rather than waiting until students have heard about all five items.

• The inventions on this page (except the letter opener) were described in "The Easy-Living Catalog of (Almost) Completely Useless Products" by D. Papia, *The Tokyo Journal*, October 1992. The electric letter opener is manufactured by Busicom Corp., Japan.

Your turn to talk

1. (Optional) Do a class brainstorm of things the students really hate to do. Write them on the board.

2. Divide the class into pairs. T: *Work in pairs. Imagine you're inventors. You're making a machine. The machine will do something you don't like to do. What will your machine do? What will it look like?*

3. As students work, circulate and help pairs having difficulty.

4. (after about 5 minutes) T: *Now join another pair. Tell your new partners about your machine.*

5. If time permits, have students form new groups of four. They tell their new partners about the machines.

Optional activity

(For use anytime during or after the unit.)

• ***Design a robot.*** Tell the students they will work in groups to design a robot that will do all the things they hate to do. They should list ten things they want the robot to do. After a few minutes, tell them there was a change in plans (such as a budget cut). Their robot can do only five things. A few minutes later, tell them there was another change. Their robot can now do only one thing. They must decide which function it is. We learned this activity from J. Harmer.

UNIT 20
Folktales

Topic/function: Appreciating folktales
Listening skills: Identifying a sequence of events (Listening Task 1); understanding and enjoying a story (Listening Task 2)
Grammar/vocabulary: Simple past

Warming Up

1. Hold your book so that students can see page 63. T: *Look at page 63.*

2. Read the introduction and the instructions. Pause when you see the symbol ♦ to give students time to answer the questions.

> *Folktales are stories that are very old.*
> *People told them for hundreds of years before anyone wrote them down.*
> *Do you know these words? Write the words on the picture.* ♦

3. After students have finished, read the second set of instructions: *Work with a partner. You will hear a story that includes the words above. What do you think the story is about?*

4. As students work, circulate and help pairs having difficulty. They don't need to write their ideas, but the story ideas should include all the items in the picture.

5. It isn't necessary to check answers, but you may want to have a few pairs share their ideas with the class. (Answers appear in black on the opposite page.)

Strategy exercise: Seeing one's own progress

Sometimes it is difficult for students to recognize their own progress. When they were beginners, everything they learned was clearly new. Now, although they are moving ahead, they may not see it because the steps they take are smaller in relation to all the English they already know. To help students see their progress over the term, choose a listening task they found challenging earlier in the course. Before they listen, have them work in pairs, listing whatever they remember about doing the activity (e.g., the speed, the vocabulary). Then play the tape. Most students will be surprised by how easy the task now is, indicating how much progress they have made.

Optional activities

(For use anytime during or after the unit.)

• *Stories we know.* Students work in pairs. Give each pair a copy of the worksheet below. Students try to identify as many folktales as possible for each picture.

Stories We Know Worksheet
Work with a partner. Look at the words. (You may use your dictionary if you don't know a word.) Can you think of famous stories that include some of these things? Write the names of the stories.

a dragon	a giant
a rabbit	gold
a castle	a wolf
a child	a king or queen
a monkey	a witch or wizard
a fairy	an important number

© Cambridge University Press

• *Twisted tales.* As a class, brainstorm names of familiar folk or fairy tales. Students work in pairs. Each pair selects a story they know and makes a "story skeleton" (an outline of events in the story like the one on page 65). Note that items should be single words and phrases, not complete sentences. When they've finished their skeleton, they change three or four things about the story. (Example: "Little Red Riding Hood was carrying a basket of food" could become "Little Blue Riding Hood was carrying a basket of books.") Pairs then join to make groups of four. They take turns telling their stories. Partners try to find the changes.

Folktales

Folktales are stories that are very old.
People told them for hundreds of years before anyone
   wrote them down.

❑ Do you know these words?
Write the words on the picture.

digging	field	~~treasure~~
farmer	playing	wheat

field ——

wheat ——

farmer

digging   playing

treasure

❑ Work with a partner.
You will hear a story that includes the words above.
What do you think the story is about?

LISTENING TASK 1

The farmer and his sons

❑ Listen. You will hear a traditional folktale.
Number the pictures (1–6).

 3

 6

 2

 5

 4

 1

In this story, there were three sons. Three is an important number in many folktales. In some stories, people have three wishes. You might know some stories with three: "The Three Goats," "The Three Little Pigs," "The Three Bears." What numbers are important in stories from your country? What other things are important?

CULTURE CORNER

64

Listening Task 1
The farmer and his sons

> **Listening skill:** Identifying a sequence of events

Note: The tapescript for Unit 20 begins on page T28.

1. T: *Look at the pictures on page 64.*

2. (Optional) Read the title: *"The farmer and his sons." What do you think this will be about?* Elicit answers from the students. (Answer: the sons growing up)

3. (Optional) If your students find listening very challenging, do the Additional Support procedure below.

4. Read the instructions: *Listen. You will hear a traditional folktale. Number the pictures, one through six.*

5. Play Listening Task 1 on the tape. Gesture for students to write the numbers.

6. If necessary, play Listening Task 1 a second time.

7. Check answers by drawing six boxes on the board to represent the pictures. Have students tell you the order. (Answers appear in blue on the opposite page.)

ADDITIONAL SUPPORT Students work in pairs. They write one or two words on each picture. The words should be whatever they think is important in the picture. OR Have students work in groups of two or three. They look at the pictures and put them in the order they think the events will occur in the story.

NOTES

• Play the entire story to let the students understand the overall idea, rather than stopping to talk about each part. If students need more time to think about what they've heard, pause the tape for a few seconds between parts.

• This lesson is based on a Sufi story from the Middle East. A good collection is *Tales of the Dervishes* by I. Shah (Penguin).

Culture corner

1. After students have read the Culture Corner, have them answer the questions in pairs or small groups: *What numbers are important in stories from your country? What other things are important?*

2. (Optional) Use this activity before students read the Culture Corner. Before class, make copies of the following worksheets. You'll need one part (A, B, or C) for each student. Divide the class into groups of three. Give each group one set of worksheets. Students read the information aloud. They listen to each other and try to decide when to say their next part. Then they read the Culture Corner to see if they were right.

Writing Worksheets

Culture corner - Part A
In this story, there // in many folk // three wishes. // some stories // goats, The three // three bears. // your country? What //

Culture corner - Part B
// sons. Three // some stories, people have // You might know // The three // What numbers // stories from // are important?

Culture corner - Part C
// were three // is an important number // tales. In // with three: // little pigs, The // are important in // other things //

© Cambridge University Press

Listening Task 2
The medicine pipe

Listening skill: Understanding and enjoying a story

1. T: *Look at page 65.*

2. **(Optional)** Read the title: *"The medicine pipe." What do you think this will be about?* Elicit answers from the students. (Answer: a Native American story)

3. **(Optional)** If your students find listening very challenging, do the Additional Support procedure below.

4. Read the introduction and the instructions: *This story is from North America. The medicine pipe is important for many Native Americans. It was a gift from their god, the Great Maker of All Things. Listen to the story of the pipe. These words will help you.*

5. Play Listening Task 2 on the tape. Gesture for students to listen and follow the outline on the left side of the page (if necessary).

6. If necessary, play Listening Task 2 a second time. Before replaying the tape, have students read the outline. Answer questions about vocabulary.

7. Read the instructions at the bottom of the page: *Did you like this story? Do you know a story like it?* Gesture for students to check "Yes" or "No."

8. **(Optional)** T: *Find a partner. Did you like the story or not? Why? What did you like? What did you dislike? Talk about the story.* (after a few minutes) *Do you know any stories like it? It could be a story of an animal that turns into something. What stories do you know?*

ADDITIONAL SUPPORT Have students read the outline in pairs and look up any words they don't know.

NOTES

• Teachers are sometimes surprised at the open-ended nature of this task. Actually, having students say whether or not they liked a story, especially if they say why, demonstrates a very high level of comprehension: appreciation. The students go far beyond simple understanding of the plot.

• Optional Step 8 asks students if they know a story like this. While this story is unique to the Sioux people, many cultures have stories about gifts from gods.

• We learned this story from Eagle Feather, a Sioux Chief in Rosebud, South Dakota, U.S.A.

Your turn to talk

1. Divide the class into groups of five. T: *Work in groups of five. You are going to tell a chain story. It can be a mystery, an adventure story, or a story about magic. One person begins. That person says the first sentence. Start like this: Once upon a time, (name) lived in (place).*

2. **(Optional)** Demonstrate with one group as the other students watch. Choose the person to begin. Prompt that student to say the first sentence, adding a name and place. Ask another student what happened next, etc.

3. T: *Someone else says the next sentence. Each person adds a new sentence to the story. Use some of the words at the bottom of the page.*

4. As students work, circulate and help groups having difficulty. If groups are having trouble getting started, give them a very strange first sentence. (Example: Once upon a time, Tom Cruise lived on the moon.)

The medicine pipe

This story is from North America. The medicine pipe is important for many Native Americans. It was a gift from their god, the Great Maker of All Things.

❏ Listen to the story of the pipe. These words will help you.

winter night
Two men lost their way.
hungry
Something moved.
a woman
food
One man ran.
steal food
fell dead
The other man watched.
The woman looked at him.
put food on the ground
He ate.
The woman sat.
body changed into a buffalo
buffalo changed into a medicine pipe
The man picked it up.
He found his way.
gift from the Great Maker

Randy Jones 95...

❏ Did you like this story?   Yes ☐   No ☐

   Do you know a story like it?   Yes ☐   No ☐

YOUR TURN TO **TALK**

Work in groups of five. You are going to tell a chain story. It can be a mystery, an adventure story, or a story about magic. One person begins. That person says the first sentence. Start like this:

Once upon a time, *(name)* lived in *(place)* .

Someone else says the next sentence. Each person adds a new sentence to the story. Use some of these words:

two sisters or brothers	a bag of gold	a forest	a bird
an old man or woman	a diamond ring	the moon	fire
a magician	the number "3"	an old house	a teacher

Activation:
a speaking and listening game

The teaching procedure for this activity begins on page T29.

The Activation game

- Work in groups of 4.
- Put a marker on "Start here."
- Close your eyes. Touch the "How many spaces?" box with a pencil. Move that many spaces.
- Read the sentences. Answer with at least 3 sentences.
- Take turns.

How many things can you say when you want someone to repeat something?

Describe a piece of clothing you bought recently.

What do you like to do on Sunday?

Start here ▶▶▶

Say three things about every member of your family.

What food don't you like?

Who is your favorite singer? What is your favorite song?

What is your favorite holiday?

How many kinds of furniture can you name in 1 minute?

Other than this class, where can you hear, read, or use English?
How many places can you think of in 1 minute?

Give directions to your favorite restaurant.

ANY PLAYER CAN ASK YOU ONE QUESTION.

Imagine you're inventing a machine. What will it do?

Do you know a song in a foreign language? What is it about?

Find 2 things (other than school) that everyone in your group does at the same time.

What is your favorite clothing store? Why do you like it?

Give directions from a well-known place to another place. Don't say where you are going. Partners, guess the place.

Start at . . .

How many different languages can you name in 1 minute?

Each person in your group says a number larger than 100. Then, everyone tries to add all the numbers.
Who is the fastest?

How many languages can you say "thank you" in?

Describe your room.

Name a story that you heard when you were a child.

Which holiday don't you like very much?

What is the most useful machine you own? Why?

What is a free-time activity that you used to do often? Choose something that you don't do now.

What is your favorite TV show? Why?

What news story is interesting to you? Why?

Who is your favorite movie star?

How many spaces?

2	1	3	1	3	2
1	3	4	2	3	1
3	1	2	1	2	3
1	2	1	3	5	2
3	5	2	1	2	3
2	1	3	4	3	1

YOU CAN ASK ANY PLAYER ONE QUESTION.

What is a typical gift in your culture?

In your group, who usually gets up the earliest on weekends? The latest?

What time do you . . .

What was your favorite toy when you were a child?

Tell about a good vacation that you've taken.

I went to . . .

What is a food you like but don't eat often. Why?

What is a good movie that you've seen? Why was it good?

I saw . . .

World map

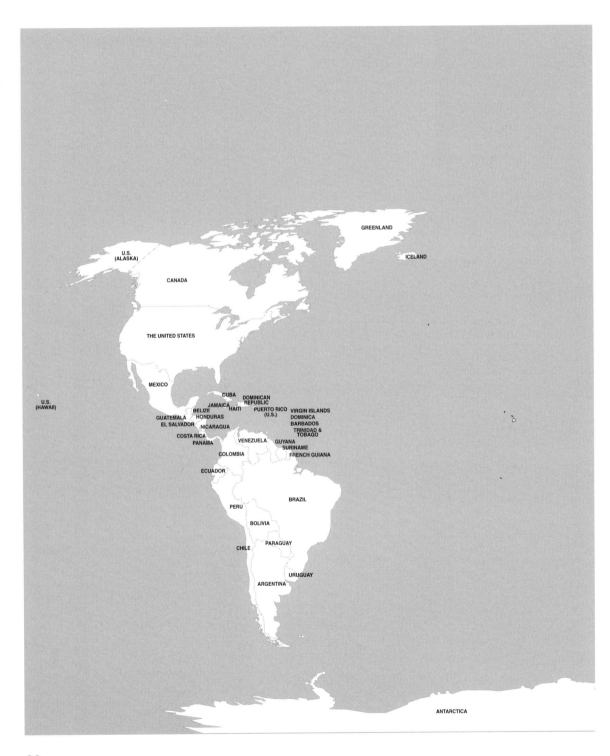

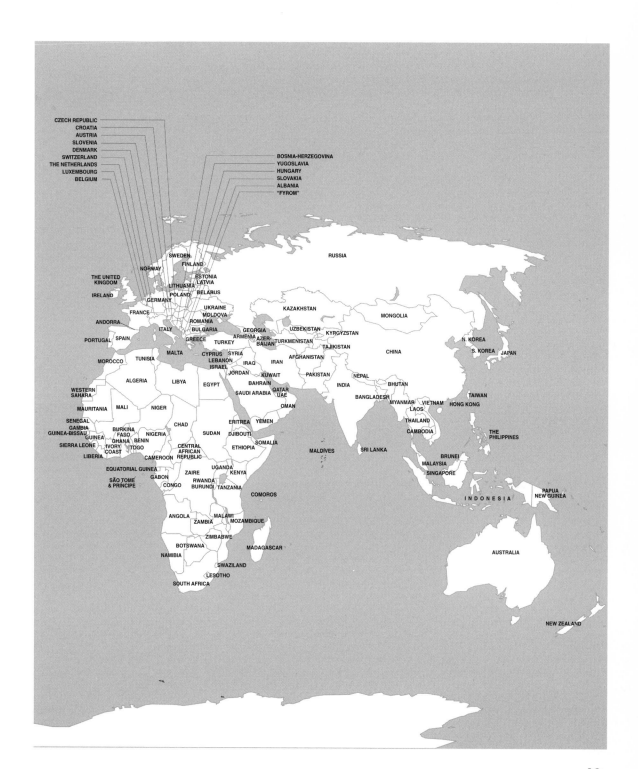

CZECH REPUBLIC
CROATIA
AUSTRIA
SLOVENIA
DENMARK
SWITZERLAND
THE NETHERLANDS
LUXEMBOURG
BELGIUM

BOSNIA-HERZEGOVINA
YUGOSLAVIA
HUNGARY
SLOVAKIA
ALBANIA
"FYROM"

SWEDEN
NORWAY
FINLAND
THE UNITED
KINGDOM
ESTONIA
LATVIA
LITHUANIA
BELARUS
IRELAND
POLAND
GERMANY
UKRAINE
FRANCE
MOLDOVA
ROMANIA
ANDORRA
ITALY
BULGARIA
PORTUGAL
SPAIN
GREECE
GEORGIA
ARMENIA AZER-
TURKEY
BAIJAN
MALTA
CYPRUS SYRIA
MOROCCO
TUNISIA
LEBANON
ISRAEL
IRAQ
JORDAN
KUWAIT
ALGERIA
LIBYA
EGYPT
BAHRAIN
QATAR
SAUDI ARABIA
UAE
WESTERN
SAHARA
OMAN
MAURITANIA
MALI
NIGER
SENEGAL
GAMBIA
BURKINA
ERITREA
YEMEN
GUINEA-BISSAU
GUINEA
FASO
NIGERIA
CHAD
SUDAN
DJIBOUTI
SIERRA LEONE
GHANA
BENIN
IVORY
TOGO
SOMALIA
LIBERIA
COAST
ETHIOPIA
CENTRAL
CAMEROON
AFRICAN
REPUBLIC
EQUATORIAL GUINEA
UGANDA
KENYA
SÃO TOMÉ
GABON
ZAIRE
& PRÍNCIPE
CONGO
RWANDA
BURUNDI
TANZANIA
COMOROS
ANGOLA
MALAWI
ZAMBIA
MOZAMBIQUE
ZIMBABWE
BOTSWANA
MADAGASCAR
NAMIBIA
SWAZILAND
LESOTHO
SOUTH AFRICA

RUSSIA

KAZAKHSTAN

MONGOLIA

UZBEKISTAN
KYRGYZSTAN
TURKMENISTAN
TAJIKISTAN
CHINA
N. KOREA
AFGHANISTAN
S. KOREA
JAPAN
IRAN
PAKISTAN
NEPAL
BHUTAN
INDIA
TAIWAN
BANGLADESH
MYANMAR
VIETNAM
HONG KONG
LAOS
THAILAND
CAMBODIA
THE
PHILIPPINES
MALDIVES
SRI LANKA
BRUNEI
MALAYSIA
SINGAPORE

INDONESIA
PAPUA
NEW GUINEA

AUSTRALIA

NEW ZEALAND

Tapescript

The following tapescript, which includes all of the listening tasks in the text, reflects *Active Listening*'s emphasis on natural, spoken English. There are, of course, differences between spoken and written English. This is a transcription of the spoken language.

You may occasionally want students to see the tapescript. For that reason, permission is granted to photocopy the script. However, the authors strongly suggest that this be done only occasionally and for specific reasons. Many students are too "word-level dependent." That is, they rely on trying to understand every word rather than overall meaning. If they insist on reading along with the script for every lesson, it can actually hurt their ability to listen and understand.

Here are two examples of situations where you might want to give out copies of the script:

• After students have completed the tasks in their text, you may want them to go back and note the uses of a particular grammatical form. In that case, you might give out the script and play the tape again, having them underline the times the form is used.

• If a class found a particular listening segment extremely difficult, you may want to give them a copy of the script. Have them read along silently as you play the tape. This increases their reading speed as well as letting them combine reading with listening to understand the segment. Then have them put away the script. Play the tape again and let them see how much they understood.

Before you begin: An introductory lesson
Learn how to listen.

Page 2. A letter from the people who wrote this book.

Listen to the letter.

READER: Dear students:

We hope that you learn a lot of English. We also hope that you enjoy learning it.

There are many different ways to learn. This book will help you learn to listen. Think about how you learn best. Find ways that work for you.

You need to be an active listener. When you listen, do these things:

1. Think about what you are listening to.
   • What is the topic?
   • What do you already know about the topic?

2. Think about what you are listening for.
   • What do you need to know?
   • What do you need to do?

3. When you don't understand, ask.
   • For example, you could say, "Could you repeat that?"

Good luck with learning English. You can do it!

Sincerely,
Marc Helgesen
Steven Brown

Page 3, Listening Task 1: Could you repeat that?

Work with a partner.

Look at the pictures.

What do you think the students are saying?
Now listen. Were you correct?

Write the sentences.

NUMBER 1

What do you say when you want someone to say something again?

FIRST WOMAN: Open your books to page 18.
SECOND WOMAN: Could you repeat that? [*pause*] Could you repeat that?
SECOND WOMAN: Excuse me? [*pause*] Excuse me?

NUMBER 2

What do you say when you want to hear the tape again?

MAN: Once more, please. [*pause*] Once more, please.

NUMBER 3

What do you say when you don't know how to spell a word?

MAN: How do you spell that? [*pause*] How do you spell that?

NUMBER 4

What do you say when you want to know a word in English?

WOMAN: How do you say that in English? [*pause*] How do you say that in English?

Page 4, Listening Task 2: Types of listening

There are many ways to listen. We listen differently for different reasons.

PART ONE: Listening for the main idea

Listen to the conversation.
What is the most important idea? Check your answer.

WOMAN: We're going out for dinner after class. Do you want to come, too?
MAN: Maybe. Where are you going?
WOMAN: Pizza King.
MAN: Pizza? I love pizza!

The answer is "dinner." They're talking about dinner.
Sometimes you don't need to understand everything you hear.
You just want the general meaning.

PART TWO: Listening for specific information

Listen again. What are they going to eat?
Check your answer.

WOMAN: We're going out for dinner after class. Do you want to come, too?
MAN: Maybe. Where are you going?
WOMAN: Pizza King.
MAN: Pizza? I love pizza!

The answer is "pizza." They're going to eat pizza.
Sometimes you only need to understand certain information.
Ask yourself, "What am I listening for?"

PART THREE: Listening "between the lines"

Listen again.
Will they go together? Check your answer.

WOMAN: We're going out for dinner after class. Do you want to come, too?
MAN: Maybe. Where are you going?
WOMAN: Pizza King.
MAN: Pizza? I love pizza!

The answer is "Yes." The man says he loves pizza.
He doesn't say "Yes, I will go with you," but you can understand his meaning.
Sometimes people don't say the exact words.
You can still understand the meaning.

Page 5, Listening Task 2: Types of listening (Continued)

Try it again. Two friends are talking on the telephone.
Each time you listen, think about the information you need.

PART ONE: Listening for the main idea

Listen. What is the most important idea?
Check your answer.

[*Phone rings; pick up*]
PAUL: Hello?
JOAN: Hi, Paul. This is Joan.
PAUL: Oh, hi. How are you feeling? Are you still sick?
JOAN: No, I feel better, thanks. I'm going to school tomorrow. What's the homework for English class?

T2

PAUL: The homework? Just a minute. . . . OK,
  here it is. Read pages 23 and 24.
JOAN: 23 and 24. OK. Thanks. See you tomorrow.
PAUL: Bye.

The answer is "school." They're talking about
school.

PART TWO: Listening for specific information

Listen. Which page numbers should she read?
Write the page numbers.

[Phone rings; pick up]
PAUL: Hello?
JOAN: Hi, Paul. This is Joan.
PAUL: Oh, hi. How are you feeling? Are you
  still sick?
JOAN: No, I feel better, thanks. I'm going to
  school tomorrow. What's the homework for
  English class?
PAUL: The homework? Just a minute. . . . OK,
  here it is. Read pages 23 and 24.
JOAN: 23 and 24. OK. Thanks. See you
  tomorrow.
PAUL: Bye.

The answer is "pages 23 and 24." Pages 23
and 24.

PART THREE: Listening "between the lines"

Listen again. Did both students go to school
today? Check your answer.

[Phone rings; pick up]
PAUL: Hello?
JOAN: Hi, Paul. This is Joan.
PAUL: Oh, hi. How are you feeling? Are you
  still sick?
JOAN: No, I feel better, thanks. I'm going to
  school tomorrow. What's the homework for
  English class?
PAUL: The homework? Just a minute. . . . OK,
  here it is. Read pages 23 and 24.
JOAN: 23 and 24. OK. Thanks. See you
  tomorrow.
PAUL: Bye.

The answer is "No." Joan was sick today. She
didn't go to school.

You heard the same conversation three times.
Each time, you listened for different reasons.
Always think about why you are listening.

Unit 1 Meeting new people

Page 7, Listening Task 1: Hello!

You're at a party. You're meeting Kent and Lisa
for the first time.
Listen to Kent.
What is your part of the conversation?
Check your answers.

NUMBER 1
[Sound of party]
KENT: This is a nice party. I'm thirsty. Uh . . .
  I'm going to get something to drink. Would
  you like something to drink? [pause] OK. Just
  a minute.

NUMBER 2
[Sound of party]
KENT: Here you are. I like this music a lot. I
  really like jazz.

NUMBER 3
[Sound of party]
KENT: I don't think we've met. My name's
  Kent. Kent Adams. [pause] It's nice to meet
  you, too.

NUMBER 4
[Sound of party]
KENT: I work at the Pine Street Library. I'm a
  librarian. How about you? What do you do?
  [pause] Oh, really. Oh, there's a friend of
  mine. Let me introduce you.

Listen. Now you are talking to Lisa.
What is your part of this conversation?
Check your answers.

NUMBER 1
LISA: This is a really nice party.

NUMBER 2
LISA: I don't think we've met. My name's Lisa.
  Lisa James.

NUMBER 3

LISA: I'm from Vancouver. I'm visiting friends here. Where are you from?

NUMBER 4

LISA: I'm thirsty. I'm going to get something to drink. Would you like something?

Page 8, Listening Task 2: Do you . . . ? Are you . . . ?

Listen. Finish the sentences.

NUMBER 1

WOMAN: Do you like jazz?

NUMBER 2

MAN: Are you from a small town?

NUMBER 3

WOMAN: Do you like tennis?

NUMBER 4

MAN: Do you like fish?

NUMBER 5

WOMAN: Are you from a big family?

NUMBER 6

MAN: Do you like dogs?

NUMBER 7

WOMAN: Are you a new student?

NUMBER 8

MAN: Do you like English?

Are these sentences true for you? Circle "yes" or "no."

Unit 2 Brothers and sisters

Page 10, Listening Task 1: Family snapshots

Listen. People are talking about their families. Which are the correct pictures?
Check your answers.

NUMBER 1

WOMAN: This is my family. I'm married. My husband's name is Bill. We have two children – a boy and a girl. Our little girl is six years old, and our little boy is four. Jennie goes to kindergarten, and Aaron goes to nursery school. My father lives with us. Grandpa's great with the kids. He loves playing with them and taking them to the park or the zoo.

NUMBER 2

MAN: This is a picture of me and my three sons. We're at a soccer game. Orlando is twelve, Luis is ten, and Carlos is nine. All three of them really like sports. Orlando and Luis play baseball. Carlos is into skating.

NUMBER 3

MAN: This is my wife June, and these are my three children. Terri on the right is the oldest. She's in high school. She's very involved in music. She's in the orchestra. Rachel – she's the one in the middle – is twelve now. And this is my son Peter. He's one year older than Rachel. Rachel and Peter are both in junior high school. Time really flies. June and I have been married for twenty years now.

NUMBER 4

WOMAN: This is a picture of me with my three kids. The girls, Jill and Anne, are both in high school. This is Jill on the right. She'll graduate next year. Anne is two years younger. My son Dan is in college. It seems like the kids are never home. I see them for dinner and sometimes on Saturday mornings, but that's about it. They're really busy and have a lot of friends.

Page 11, Listening Task 2: Your family tree

You're going to write about your family. You need to know these shapes:
star, square, diamond, circle.
Listen. Write your answers.

NUMBER 1

WOMAN: Start with yourself. Find the star, in the middle of the page. Write your name in the star. In the star, write your name. When is your birthday? Write it in the star, under your name. Under your name, write your birthday.

NUMBER 2

MAN: Find the square. The square is for your father. Write your father's name in the square. In the square, write your father's name. Where was your father born? Write it in the square, under his name. Under your father's name, write his birthplace.

NUMBER 3

WOMAN: Now find the diamond. It's next to the square. Write your mother's name in the diamond. In the diamond, write your mother's name. Where was your mother born? Write her birthplace in the diamond, under her name. Your mother's name and place of birth go in the diamond. Your father's name and place of birth go in the square.

NUMBER 4

MAN: Do you have brothers and sisters? Are your brothers and sisters older than you or younger than you? Write the names of your older brothers and sisters in the green circles. How old are they? Write the ages of your older brothers and sisters under their names.

NUMBER 5

WOMAN: Do you have younger brothers and sisters? Write the names of your younger brothers and sisters in the blue circles. How old are they? Under their names, write the ages of your younger brothers and sisters.

Unit 3 Numbers

Page 13, Listening Task 1: Information

Listen. People want to know the telephone numbers for places in these cities. Write the telephone numbers.

NUMBER 1: Sydney, Australia

[*Phone rings; pick up*]

WOMAN: Directory Assistance.

MAN: I'd like the number of the Hilton International Hotel in Sydney, please.

WOMAN: Just a moment. The one on Pitt Street?

MAN: That's right.

WOMAN: The number is (02) 266-0610.

MAN: 266-0610. Thank you. Oh . . . that's area code 02?

WOMAN: Yes. Area code 02.

NUMBER 2: São Paulo, Brazil

[*Phone rings; pick up*]

MAN: Front desk. How may I help you?

WOMAN: I need the number for the United States Consulate in São Paulo.

MAN: The city code for São Paulo is 11. Just a minute for that number. The number of the United States Consulate is 881-6511.

WOMAN: So I dial 11-881-6511?

MAN: Yes. 11-881-6511.

NUMBER 3: Tokyo, Japan

[*Phone rings; pick up*]

WOMAN: United States Embassy.

MAN: What time does the American Center Library open?

WOMAN: The American Center is in a different building, sir. The number for the library is 3436-0901.

MAN: 3436-0901? Thank you.

NUMBER 4: Toronto, Canada

[*Phone rings; pick up*]

MAN: Directory Assistance.

WOMAN: Yes. I'd like to buy baseball tickets – Toronto Blue Jays baseball tickets. I need the phone number of their ticket office, please.

MAN: The Blue Jays' number is 341-1234.

WOMAN: And the area code is 416?

MAN: That's right. (416) 341-1234.

NUMBER 5: Kuala Lumpur, Malaysia

[*Phone rings; pick up*]

WOMAN: Front desk.

MAN: Could I have the number of the Tourist Development Center, please?

WOMAN: The Tourist Development Center is 293-5188.

MAN: 293-5188. Thanks.

NUMBER 6: Mexico City, Mexico

[*Phone rings; pick up*]

WOMAN: Front desk.

MAN: Could I have the number for Continental Airlines, please?

WOMAN: Just a minute. Yes. It's 203-9444.
MAN: 203-9444. Thank you.
WOMAN: You're quite welcome.

Page 14, Listening Task 2: The Champions!

Listen. These teams are in a basketball tournament. Write the scores.
Which team wins each game?
Write the first letter of the team's name in the circle.

[*Music*]

MAN: Hello, sports fans, and welcome to "This Week's Sports." The big news this week, of course, is the basketball championship. It started on Friday. The Lions beat the Hawks, ninety-four to sixty-eight. That score again: The Lions won. Lions ninety-four, Hawks sixty-eight. [*pause*]

Things were closer with the Tigers and the Eagles. The Eagles won. They won by just four points. The score: one hundred and three to ninety-nine. Again, the Eagles one-oh-three, the Tigers ninety-nine. [*pause*]

Next, the Panthers played the Bears. The Panthers won over the Bears, eighty-seven to seventy-three. The Panthers eighty-seven, the Bears seventy-three. [*pause*]

And in the last game, the Rockets beat the Comets. The Rockets won, seventy-two to sixty-five. Rockets seventy-two, Comets sixty-five. [*pause*]

Then on Saturday, we saw some real action. It was the Lions against the Eagles. And the Lions won, with ninety-two points. The Eagles had eighty points. The score: Lions ninety-two, Eagles eighty. [*pause*]

And in the other big game on Saturday, the Rockets beat the Panthers one hundred and seven to eighty-six. The Rockets won. Rockets one-oh-seven, Panthers eighty-six. [*pause*]

That brings us to the championship game on Sunday. It was the Lions against the Rockets. It was a good game. And in the end, the Rockets won; they had one hundred and nine

points. The Lions had ninety-eight. So the new champions are the Rockets. Rockets one-oh-nine, Lions ninety-eight. [*pause*]

That's it for basketball action. Turning now to the excitement of professional bowling . . .

Unit 4 Let's eat!

Page 16, Listening Task 1: This tastes great!

Listen. People are eating different foods. They don't say the names of the foods.
What are they talking about?
Number the pictures (1–6). There are two extra pictures.

NUMBER 1

[*Sound of park*]
MAN: Do you want chocolate or vanilla?
WOMAN: Uh . . . chocolate, I guess.
MAN: Here you go.
WOMAN: Thanks. Hmm . . . this tastes great. Nothing like it on a hot day!

NUMBER 2

[*Sound of doorbell; followed by door being opened*]
FIRST WOMAN: Hi.
MAN: Here is it. That's $12.50.
FIRST WOMAN: Here you go. Keep the change.
MAN: Thanks.
[*sound of door closing*]
FIRST WOMAN: It's here.
SECOND WOMAN: Great. You ordered a big one?
FIRST WOMAN: Yeah. The fourteen-inch size.
SECOND WOMAN: What toppings?
FIRST WOMAN: Let's see . . . there are mushrooms, onions, black olives, green peppers, and extra cheese.
SECOND WOMAN: Sounds great. I'll get some soda from the fridge.

NUMBER 3

FIRST MAN: Do you use cream or sugar?
SECOND MAN: No. Just black.
FIRST MAN: There's more when you finish. I made a whole pot.

SECOND MAN: Great. I'm not human without a cup in the morning.
FIRST MAN: I know what you mean.

NUMBER 4

MAN: So you made this yourself?
WOMAN: Yeah. I'm taking a class in Japanese cooking. It's pretty easy to make.
MAN: How do you get the rice to stick together?
WOMAN: Oh, it's the kind of rice. You need to use short-grain rice. It's kind of sticky. You mix the rice with a little vinegar and sugar. You just stick it together with your hands and put a piece of raw fish on it. I especially like shrimp. A lot of people like octopus, but I'm not crazy about it.
MAN: Gee, this is really good.

NUMBER 5

WOMAN: This looks interesting.
MAN: Yeah. That's what they use to eat curry.
WOMAN: To eat curry?
MAN: Right. You don't use a spoon. Instead, you just tear off a piece of this and dip it into the curry.
WOMAN: I've never had this before. It's good.
MAN: You can eat it with lots of different Indian food – not just curry.

NUMBER 6

WOMAN: This is really good.
MAN: You want some lemon on it? Or tartar sauce?
WOMAN: No, it's just fine this way.
MAN: Watch out for the bones. There are a lot of little bones.
WOMAN: No problem.
MAN: I caught them myself, you know.
WOMAN: Really? You caught all these?
MAN: Yeah. I was up at the lake last weekend.
WOMAN: At the lake? So that's where you got that suntan.

MAN: Yeah. I spent all day Saturday in my boat. I caught quite a few.
WOMAN: Hmmm . . . a day on the lake sounds nice.

Page 17, Listening Task 2: How about a pizza?

Listen. Some friends are deciding where to go to dinner.
Cross out the places where they don't want to eat.
Circle the place they choose. There is one extra place.

FIRST WOMAN: OK. I guess we're finished.
MAN: I'm tired. Let's go out to dinner.
FIRST WOMAN: Good idea. I don't want to cook. Maya, do you want to go with us?
SECOND WOMAN: Where are you going?
MAN: Well, let's see. There's a new Mexican restaurant near here.
FIRST WOMAN: I went there last week. I love Mexican food, but that restaurant . . . well, um . . .
MAN: It's not very good, huh?
FIRST WOMAN: No. Let's go someplace else. [pause] I know! There's Indian Garden. They have really good Indian food. Hey, Maya, have you ever had Indian food?
SECOND WOMAN: Sure. There are lots of Indian restaurants in my country. But I don't like spicy food too much.
FIRST WOMAN: Well, this place has really spicy food. I guess we can't go to Indian Garden.
SECOND WOMAN: Sorry.
FIRST WOMAN: No, that's OK. [pause]
MAN: Let's see. Can't go to the Mexican place. Can't go to the Indian restaurant.
FIRST WOMAN: Pizza!
MAN: Oh, come on! We had pizza last night. And Sunday night, too.
FIRST WOMAN: Yeah, I guess we *have* been eating a lot of pizza.

MAN: Pizza's great, but not tonight.
FIRST WOMAN: OK, no pizza. [*pause*]
SECOND WOMAN: I have an idea. Let's go to The Steak Place.
FIRST WOMAN: The Steak Place? That's boring: steak, potatoes, salad.
MAN: Meat and potatoes. Just like my mother cooks.
SECOND WOMAN: Oh, but I love steak. I could eat it every day. Come on. Let's go!
FIRST WOMAN: Well, I guess that *would* be OK.
MAN: Yeah, I guess so. Hmm . . . I haven't had steak in a long time.
SECOND WOMAN: Come on. I'm hungry.

Unit 5 Your free time

Page 19, Listening Task 1: How often?

Listen. These people are talking about their free-time activities.
How often do they do these things?
Draw lines to show how often.

NUMBER 1
[*Sound of busy street*]
FIRST MAN: How often do you read magazines after dinner?
SECOND MAN: Read magazines after dinner? I read them often. I'd say five or six nights a week. I usually read news magazines. There's also a science magazine I like a lot.

NUMBER 2
[*Sound of busy street*]
MAN: Do you play a sport on weekends?
WOMAN: Sometimes.
MAN: How often?
WOMAN: About twice a month. I play tennis. Sometimes I go swimming, too.

NUMBER 3
[*Sound of busy street*]
MAN: Is anyone here studying a foreign language?
WOMAN: I am. I'm studying Chinese.

MAN: How often do you study at night?
WOMAN: Hardly ever. I'm tired in the evenings – after work and all. I try to study a little bit every morning. I feel fresher then. Weekends too. My class is on Saturday. But I don't study at night very often.

NUMBER 4
[*Sound of busy street*]
FIRST MAN: Do you watch TV on Saturday night?
SECOND MAN: No, never. Not on Saturday night. I usually meet friends . . . maybe go dancing, see a movie, something like that. But watch TV? That would be a waste of the weekend.

NUMBER 5
[*Sound of busy street*]
FIRST MAN: Do you go to a restaurant for lunch very often?
SECOND MAN: Yeah, every day. There are several restaurants in the building where I work. The prices are good. It's just easier than bringing my lunch.

NUMBER 6
[*Sound of busy street*]
MAN: Do you listen to music in the evening?
WOMAN: Most of the time. Maybe five nights a week. I usually listen to the radio or watch the music channel on TV. I really like music.

Page 20, Listening Task 2: Which is more popular?

People in the United States spend their free time in different ways.
Look at the questions. What do you think the answers will be?
Check your answers.
Now listen. Circle the correct answers.
Write at least one extra fact about each item.

NUMBER 1
WOMAN: OK, you get the first question. Do more people enjoy classical, country and western, or rock music?
MAN: Gee, uh . . . rock, I guess.

WOMAN: No, actually more people like country and western. Fifty-nine percent like country music. Only forty-four percent say they like rock.

MAN: Fifty-nine percent like country? I'm surprised. How about classical?

WOMAN: That was only forty percent.

MAN: Wait! That's more than a hundred percent.

WOMAN: Yeah, but the question asked if they like the music. You can like more than one type.

MAN: Oh, I guess so.

NUMBER 2

FIRST MAN: I get the next question.

SECOND MAN: Why do most people listen to the radio, for news or for entertainment?

FIRST MAN: I listen for the news, so I'll guess that.

SECOND MAN: You're right. Ninety-two percent listen to the radio for the news. Only eighty-eight percent listen for enjoyment.

NUMBER 3

MAN: My question.

WOMAN: OK. What type of magazines do more people read, TV guides or news magazines?

MAN: News magazines? All of them?

WOMAN: Yeah. *Time, Newsweek* . . . all of them.

MAN: I guess I'd say . . . TV guides.

WOMAN: You're right. TV guides sell about 17 million copies a week. The news magazines only sell 10 million.

MAN: Maybe people are watching the news on TV.

NUMBER 4

FIRST WOMAN: OK, your turn. Which sport is more popular, swimming or jogging?

SECOND WOMAN: Jogging? It's easier to do.

FIRST WOMAN: No, more people like swimming. About seventeen percent.

SECOND WOMAN: Seventy?

FIRST WOMAN: No, seven<u>teen</u>. One-seven. But only about thirteen percent go running.

NUMBER 5

WOMAN: Here's the last question. Which is true of more people: They never exercise in their free time, or they like to be active?

MAN: People who never exercise or who like to be active? I don't know. I'd guess more people never exercise.

WOMAN: Wrong. Only twenty-five percent say they never exercise. Forty percent say they'd rather be active during their free time.

MAN: Really . . . more people like to be active. Huh. I wouldn't have guessed. Hey, Jim, can you bring me another soda?

Unit 6 That's a nice shirt.

Page 22, Listening Task 1: What are they wearing?

Listen. What are Anna and Mike wearing today? Circle your answers.

WOMAN: This is Anna. She's wearing a pair of white pants today. Her white pants are new. Today's the first time she's worn them. [*pause*] She's wearing a striped blouse. The blouse has short sleeves. She's wearing a short-sleeved striped blouse. [*pause*] Anna's also wearing a baseball cap. She loves baseball and likes to wear her favorite team's cap. [*pause*] Anna's not wearing a jacket today. It's too warm for a jacket. [*pause*] She's carrying a bag today. It's a very large bag – big enough to hold her tennis racket and tennis balls. Anna's playing tennis today.

MAN: This is Mike. He's wearing dark blue pants. Mike often wears dark pants – either black or blue. [*pause*] He's wearing a white shirt – a plain white shirt. Mike's wearing a nice white shirt. [*pause*] Mike's also wearing a tie – a tie with stripes on it. He's wearing a shirt and a striped tie. [*pause*] He's also wearing a dark blue jacket. The dark blue jacket matches his dark pants. Mike's wearing a suit – dark pants, dark jacket. [*pause*] Mike doesn't usually dress like this. He's going to a wedding today. His friends are getting married, so he's getting dressed up.

Page 23, Listening Task 2: Dressing for work

Listen. On Fridays, people in Dan's office wear casual clothes to work.

Dan is explaining why. Check his reasons.

NUMBER 1: With casual clothes . . .

[*Sound of busy street*]

WOMAN: Hey Dan, where are you going?

DAN: I'm going to work.

WOMAN: To work? Look at you. You're not wearing a suit. You're wearing . . . well, just regular clothes.

DAN: We don't have to wear suits on Fridays anymore. There are new rules at work. We can wear whatever we want.

WOMAN: That's great!

DAN: Yeah. And believe it or not, casual clothes are good for the environment.

WOMAN: Good for the environment? Stopping pollution?

DAN: Yeah. Casual clothes actually stop pollution.

WOMAN: How?

DAN: Well, people don't dry-clean casual clothes. You have to dry-clean suits. Dry cleaning uses chemicals. Some chemicals are bad for the environment.

WOMAN: Fewer chemicals. I never thought of that.

NUMBER 2: At the office . . .

DAN: When we wear casual clothes, they turn down the air conditioner in the office. We don't wear jackets. We aren't so warm. We don't need as much air conditioning. Less air conditioning uses less electricity . . . helps the environment.

WOMAN: Less air conditioning. Hmm.

NUMBER 3: Getting to work . . .

DAN: The best thing about casual clothes is that I can ride my bicycle to work. I can't ride my bicycle in a suit. I'd get too hot. But now I ride my bicycle on Friday. I don't drive my car . . . less pollution.

WOMAN: Gee, casual clothes really are good for the environment.

DAN: And they feel good, too.

Unit 7 Furniture and houses

Page 25, Listening Task 1: What are they talking about?

People are talking about furniture and other things in houses.

What are they talking about? Number the pictures (1–5).

There are four extra pictures.

NUMBER 1

[*Doorbell; door opening followed by door closing; click of an electric switch*]

WOMAN: This one looks nice.

MAN: Yeah. There's a lot of room in the top part.

WOMAN: We can put glasses, cups, dishes – that sort of thing – on the top shelves.

MAN: Right. And the bottom would be good for pots and pans.

WOMAN: I think this one's just right.

NUMBER 2

MAN: So how do you like this one?

WOMAN: I like it. It's really comfortable. Try it.

MAN: It does feel good. And three people can sit on it.

WOMAN: That will help when friends come over.

MAN: I think we should get it.

NUMBER 3

[*Doorbell; door opens*]

FIRST WOMAN: Oh, hi, Sue. Come on in.
[*door closes*]

SECOND WOMAN: Thanks. Gee, it sure feels good in here. So cool.

FIRST WOMAN: Yeah. I just bought it last week. I really only need it about two months a year.

SECOND WOMAN: But when it's hot out, it's really hot. Like today.

FIRST WOMAN: Sit down, relax, and cool off. I'll get you some iced tea.

SECOND WOMAN: That would be great.

NUMBER 4

FIRST MAN: No place to sit. Just a minute. I'll get one from the closet. [*pause*]

SECOND MAN: This is convenient.

FIRST MAN: I have two of them . . . for when people come over. I like them. They're comfortable. And I can fold them up and put them away – put them in the closet when I don't need them.

SECOND MAN: That's a good idea.

NUMBER 5

MAN: That's nice. Is it new?

WOMAN: Uh-huh. I just got it a couple months ago.

MAN: I like the design.

WOMAN: So do I. But I really like how bright it is. I bought it for reading. [*click of an electric switch*]

MAN: It *is* bright.

WOMAN: 150 watts . . . perfect for reading.

Page 26, Listening Task 2: Where's the heater?

Around the world, people keep their houses warm in different ways.

Listen. Where are the heaters in these rooms? Circle them. If there is no heater, check none.

NUMBER 1: Syria

WOMAN: People think the Middle East is very warm . . . and it is. But it can get cold during the winter. I visited my grandparents in Syria last winter. Boy, it was really cold for about a week. Fortunately, they had a great heater. Many people there use oil to heat their homes. Some houses have a large heater that heats the whole house. My grandparents' house had a heater in the living room.

NUMBER 2: Germany

MAN: In Germany, some houses have a heater called a *kachelofen* In this house, it's in the living room. The *kachelofen* has a metal door. The front is covered with tiles. Wood is burned inside the *kachelofen* The tiles get very warm. After the wood has burned for a week, the *kachelofen* heats for two or three more days.

NUMBER 3: Korea

WOMAN: I used to live in Korea. It can get really cold during the winter, but the house I lived in had an *ondol* floor. That's a floor with pipes in it. The pipes carry the heat. They heat up the whole floor. We sat on cushions on the floor. The entire floor was a heater.

NUMBER 4: Brazil

MAN: Brazil is a warm country. We don't usually need heaters. Check "none" for this picture.

NUMBER 5: Japan

WOMAN: I loved living in Japan. They have this kind of heater called a *kotatsu*. It's electric. It's in a low table, under the tabletop. When you sit at the table, the *kotatsu* keeps your legs warm. Of course, there are other ways to stay warm. Most houses have kerosene stoves. Now, many people use electric carpets, too.

Unit 8 How do you start your day?

Page 28, Listening Task 1: And after that?

Listen to these people. In what order do they do things?

Write the numbers (1–3).

There is one extra item for each.

NUMBER 1: What does Eric do in the morning?

ERIC: I usually get up at about seven. The first thing I do is take a shower. And let's see. . . . After I take a shower, I eat breakfast. When I finish breakfast, I usually read the newspaper. I only have about twenty minutes to read the paper. Then I have to leave for school.

NUMBER 2: What does Anne do in the morning?

ANNE: I make coffee as soon as I get up. I really need my cup of coffee in the morning. I don't eat breakfast – I just have a cup of coffee. Anyway, after that I usually exercise. I like lifting weights for fifteen or twenty minutes. Then I've got to go to work. I have to be at the office by about nine.

NUMBER 3: What does Karen do after school?

KAREN: After class, I usually study. I like to finish all my homework – reading, everything – before I eat dinner. So, yeah, I study and then eat dinner. And after that I usually watch TV. I like watching the news and maybe a movie or a drama . . . or something.

NUMBER 4: What does Joel do in the evening?

JOEL: I get home from work at about seven, so we eat dinner right away. After dinner, it's time for my children to go to bed. I usually put them to bed at about . . . uh . . . about eight o'clock. Then what? Usually I just read. I read to relax. I enjoy it.

Page 29, Listening Task 2: And then I . . .

Think about yesterday. What did you do?
You are going to write about your day. Listen. Write your answers.

NUMBER 1

WOMAN: Think about yesterday. What time did you wake up? Was it early or late? Did you wake up at your usual time? Write the time you woke up yesterday.

NUMBER 2

MAN: After you woke up, what did you do? Did you eat breakfast? What did you eat? Think about yesterday. Write down the things you ate for breakfast. If you didn't eat breakfast, just write "no."

NUMBER 3

WOMAN: OK, now think about yesterday morning. What did you do? Did you go outside? Did you go to work? Did you stay at home? Write down two things you did yesterday morning. They don't have to be special things. Just write down two things you did.

NUMBER 4

MAN: What about the afternoon? Did you have a good time? Did you do anything special? Did you work? Write down one thing you did in the afternoon. Write down just one thing.

NUMBER 5

WOMAN: Did you have a good evening? What did you do last night? Where did you go? Did you eat anything special? Write down something you did last night. Write down as many things as you can.

NUMBER 6

MAN: Finally, write down the time you went to bed. What time did you go to bed last night? Was it early or late? Write down the time.

Unit 9 I'd like to see that!

Page 31, Listening Task 1: Let's go!

Listen. Some friends are talking about movies. Are they going to see the movies together? Check "yes" or "no."

NUMBER 1

[Sound of busy street]
JEFF: Hi, Carl. What's up?
CARL: Hey, Jeff. We're on our way to see that new comedy Running From the Mob. Want to go with us?
JEFF: I hear it's really funny.
CARL: Yeah, it's got a lot of good people in it. Should be great. Let's go.
JEFF: Ah, I wish I could, but I've got to study.
CARL: Well, maybe next time. You're missing a good thing.
JEFF: I know. Got to go. See you.
CARL: Bye.

NUMBER 2

[Phone rings; pick up]
SALLY: Hello?
RAY: Sally?
SALLY: Yes?
RAY: This is Ray.

SALLY: Oh, hi, Ray. How are you?

RAY: Fine. How about you? It's been a long time.

SALLY: Yes, I guess it has.

RAY: Uh . . . would you like to go to a movie tonight? *Friday the 13th, Part 17* is playing.

SALLY: *Friday the 13th?* Great! I'm in the mood for a good horror movie. Hey, didn't we see Part 1 together?

RAY: You know, I think we did. OK. I'll pick you up at 7:45?

SALLY: Sure. See you then.

NUMBER 3

[*Sound of busy street*]

BILL: Jim! Just the man I wanted to see.

JIM: Hi, Bill. You look excited.

BILL: I am. Do you know what starts at the Regent tonight?

JIM: No, I'm afraid I don't.

BILL: *Godzilla 2010* – that's what.

JIM: Huh?

BILL: The new Godzilla movie!

JIM: I didn't know they made them anymore.

BILL: Oh, yeah. I still love them. Want to go?

JIM: Gee, Bill, I have a lot to do around the house.

BILL: Come on. You'll love it.

JIM: Not tonight. Maybe some other time.

NUMBER 4

FIRST WOMAN: Let's do something this weekend.

SECOND WOMAN: Yeah, I'm bored.

FIRST WOMAN: How about a movie? Maybe a classic. The Oak Theater has a couple of old love stories.

SECOND WOMAN: That sounds good. I love old movies. They don't make them like they used to.

FIRST WOMAN: That's for sure.

NUMBER 5

MAN: Oh, there's a musical on TV tonight . . . after the news!

WOMAN: It's 11:30. I have to work tomorrow.

MAN: Well, I don't.

WOMAN: Go ahead and watch it. I'm going to bed.

MAN: Oh, come on! It'll be great.

WOMAN: I'm going to sleep. Good night!

NUMBER 6

WOMAN: Let's see what's playing at the movies. Ah, here. Arnold's back!

MAN: Oh, another violent action movie?

WOMAN: No. This one's funny.

MAN: But it's still an action movie, right?

WOMAN: Well, yeah, but . . .

MAN: I don't like violence, and I won't pay to watch it.

WOMAN: Oh, come on.

MAN: Sorry.

Page 32, Listening Task 2: A night at the movies

Film critics watch movies.

They tell people if the films are good or bad.

Listen. What kinds of movies are the film critics talking about?

Check them.

Do the critics like the films?

Write "yes" or "no."

NUMBER 1: Beyond the Stars

[*Music*]

JEAN: Good evening and welcome to "A Night at the Movies." I'm Jean Channing.

ROBERT: And I'm Robert Evans. Tonight we're going to look at this week's new films, starting with *Beyond the Stars*.

JEAN: *Beyond the Stars* is a good movie. It's full of rockets and lights and lots of other special effects. It's the story of a space flight to Mars that gets into trouble. Another team of astronauts saves the crew. These astronauts are a mix of aliens, robots, and people – just like in the *Star Wars* movies.

ROBERT: I liked it, too. The special effects are wonderful. Go see this movie.

NUMBER 2: Another Fine Mess

JEAN: Next we have *Another Fine Mess*. This is the funniest movie you will see all year. If you like a lot of jokes and silly situations, this is the movie for you. You'll laugh the entire time. This one is a "must see."

ROBERT: I really don't agree. Yes, there are some laughs, but I thought the story was stupid. There was nothing new. It's a bad movie.

NUMBER 3: My Guy

JEAN: Well, Robert, I think we will agree on *My Guy*. It's one everyone really should go to. The rock songs are great, and the dancing's great, too.

ROBERT: I liked *My Guy* a lot. I usually don't like rock music, but I liked this movie. Why? Well, it had a real story. Don't miss it.

NUMBER 4: Crack Up

JEAN: I didn't like this next movie, *Crack Up*. Car chases, car crashes, fights . . . this is a noisy, nasty, violent movie. It's about two police officers who are old friends. When one needs help, the other joins him. The men travel across the country, looking for criminals and boring the audience.

ROBERT: I agree. It's a bad movie from beginning to end. I really hated it.

NUMBER 5: Just You and Me

JEAN: Our last movie is called *Just You and Me*. Two teenagers meet at school. At first, they don't like each other. Then things change. When the girl's family moves to another city, the boy runs away from home to be near her. They must meet secretly, just like in *Romeo and Juliet* – only this movie isn't as good as *Romeo and Juliet*. In fact, it's pretty bad.

ROBERT: I didn't like this movie. It's an old story, and they just don't do anything new with it.

JEAN: Well, that's all the time we have for tonight. Thanks for watching.

ROBERT: See you next week. Good night.

T14

Unit 10 Where is it?

Page 34, Listening Task 1: I'm lost!

Listen. People are looking for places. Where are the places? Check the correct circles.

NUMBER 1 The Four Seasons Restaurant

[*Sound of busy street*]

WOMAN: Excuse me. I'm looking for the Four Seasons Restaurant. I was supposed to meet someone there an hour ago. I can't find it.

MAN: The Four Seasons? Well, you're almost there. It's just around the corner.

WOMAN: Around the corner?

MAN: Yeah. It's in the middle of the block. Just turn left at the corner. It's on your left, just past the coffee shop.

WOMAN: Around the corner, just past the coffee shop. Thank you.

MAN: You're welcome.

NUMBER 2: The Century Hotel

[*Sound of busy street*]

MAN: Excuse me, Officer.

OFFICER: Yes?

MAN: I'm looking for the Century Hotel.

OFFICER: The Century Hotel. That's two blocks from here.

MAN: Two blocks from here?

OFFICER: Yeah. Walk two blocks and turn left. You'll see the hotel on the right. The hotel is next to a drugstore.

MAN: On the right?

OFFICER: Yes. It's next to a drugstore . . . and across the street from a bank.

MAN: Next to a drugstore, across from a bank.

OFFICER: You got it.

NUMBER 3: a drugstore

[*Sound of busy street*]

FIRST WOMAN: [*cough*]

SECOND WOMAN: You OK?

FIRST WOMAN: I'm getting a cold. I think I should get some cold medicine.

SECOND WOMAN: There's a drugstore on the next block.

FIRST WOMAN: Really? I don't remember one.

SECOND WOMAN: Walk straight ahead and turn left. It's new . . . right next to Holiday Travel.

FIRST WOMAN: Next to Holiday Travel? Oh, across from that supermarket.

SECOND WOMAN: Right.

FIRST WOMAN: OK. I'll check it out.

NUMBER 4: a video store

[*Sounds of busy street*]

MAN: Hey, they just opened a new video store a block from here. It's great. They have a huge selection . . . thousands and thousands of videos.

WOMAN: Yeah? Where is it?

MAN: Walk one block and turn right at the light. You know that shoe store? The big one?

WOMAN: Payright Shoes. Yeah, I know it.

MAN: Well, the video store is right across from that.

WOMAN: Oh. By the flower shop?

MAN: Yeah, between the flower shop and that software place.

WOMAN: Let's stop by and see what they've got.

Page 35, Listening Task 2: Safari Park

Safari Park is a zoo. There are no cages.
Listen to the tour of Safari Park. Where are the places?
Write the numbers on the map (1–6). There is one extra place on the map.
1. The Life Science Center 2. The Brazilian Rain Forest 3. The Children's Zoo 4. Monkey Mountain 5. Lion Land 6. The Gift Shop

WOMAN: Good morning, ladies and gentlemen. Welcome to Safari Park. When you go along the walkway, you'll see the beautiful animals of the park – all in their natural environment. [*pause*]

First, you'll see the Animals of Asia to your right. Just past the Asian animals, you'll find Flamingo Pond. We're sure you'll like the beautiful pink birds. [*pause*]

Continue along the walkway. On your right, you will see the wild animals of the North American Prairie. After that, it's Monkey Mountain where you'll notice the baby monkeys playing. That's Monkey Mountain, between the North American Prairie and Bear Country. [*pause*]

Just after Bear Country is the Children's Zoo. Children of all ages can hold and pet the rabbits, sheep, and other animals in the Children's Zoo – between Bear Country and the Craft Center. The Craft Center features items from many parts of the world. [*pause*]

Follow the path and cross the bridge over the Crocodile River. Continue around the corner. To your left is Elephant Island. To your right is Lion Land. There are over seventy African lions in Lion Land, just across the Crocodile River. [*pause*]

After Lion Land, cross the Crocodile River again. Continue along the walkway. You'll see the largest part of Safari Park on your left. This is the Brazilian Rain Forest. The Rain Forest goes from the Crocodile River all the way down to the World Restaurant. [*pause*]

All of us at Safari Park believe in taking care of the environment. Be sure to spend time at the Life Science Center, right across from the Rain Forest. The Life Science Center is between the World Restaurant and the film shop. The Life Science Center is both educational and interesting. You will learn more about the environment. [*pause*]

When you leave the Life Science Center, you're almost at the end of your visit. But before you go home, don't miss Animals of the Night. Bats, owls, and other animals are waiting for you. And, of course, you'll want to stop by the gift shop. The gift shop is next to Animals of the Night, between Animals of the Night and the park entrance. [*pause*]

We hope you enjoy your visit to Safari Park. We hope you enjoy seeing some of the beautiful animals that share the earth with us.

Unit 11 The Midnight Special

Page 37, Listening Task 1: What's the story?

Listen to the song.
Number the pictures (1–4).
SINGER: Oh, let the Midnight Special
  Shine a light on me.
  Oh, let the Midnight Special
  Shine an ever-loving light on me.
  If you ever get to Houston,
  You'd better act right.
  You'd better not gamble,
  And you'd better not fight.
  The sheriff will arrest you.
  He's going to take you down.
  The next thing you know is
  That you're jailhouse bound.
  (Chorus)
  Every Monday morning
  When the big bell rings,
  You go to the table,
  You see the same old things.
  Not much food on the table,
  Just some bread in a pan.
  If you say anything about it,
  You get in trouble with the man.
  (Chorus)
  Here comes Miss Rosy.
  Oh, how can you tell?
  By the umbrella on her shoulder,
  She's such a good-looking gal.
  A straw hat is on her head,
  Piece of paper in her hand.
  She wants to see the jailer,
  She wants to free her man.
  (Chorus)

Page 38, Listening Task 2: Catch the rhythm.

Listen to the song again.
Underline the stressed (loudest) syllables.
SINGER: Oh, let the Midnight Special
  Shine a light on me.
  Oh, let the Midnight Special
  Shine an ever-loving light on me.

  If you ever get to Houston,
  You'd better act right.
  You'd better not gamble,
  And you'd better not fight.
  The sheriff will arrest you.
  He's going to take you down.
  The next thing you know is
  That you're jailhouse bound.
  (Chorus)
  Every Monday morning
  When the big bell rings,
  You go to the table,
  You see the same old things.
  Not much food on the table,
  Just some bread in a pan.
  If you say anything about it,
  You get in trouble with the man.
  (Chorus)
  Here comes Miss Rosy.
  Oh, how can you tell?
  By the umbrella on her shoulder,
  She's such a good-looking gal.
  A straw hat is on her head,
  Piece of paper in her hand.
  She wants to see the jailer,
  She wants to free her man.
  (Chorus)

Unit 12 Gifts and greetings

Page 40, Listening Task 1: Gifts and cultures

People in all countries enjoy gifts.
Sometimes the meanings are different in other cultures.
Listen. Which item is not a good gift? Cross out the picture.
Why not? Check your answer.

NUMBER 1: China
WOMAN: Did I tell you I'm going to China?
MAN: China? Great.
WOMAN: Yes. I'm going to Shanghai on business. I have to buy some gifts.
MAN: Good idea. What are you going to bring?
WOMAN: I was thinking of bringing some

handkerchiefs. They're colorful, beautiful . . . also lightweight. I don't want to carry anything heavy.

MAN: Ah, I don't think you should give handkerchiefs. They aren't a good gift in Chinese culture.

WOMAN: Why not?

MAN: A handkerchief is a symbol of saying goodbye.

WOMAN: Saying goodbye?

MAN: Yeah, like when you're going away . . . and people are crying, so they need a handkerchief. Actually, I've heard that one of the best things to give is a dinner – not a present, but a big dinner. It's good for business.

NUMBER 2: *Argentina*

WOMAN: This is interesting. Did you know that in Argentina you should never give clothing unless you know the person really well?

MAN: Don't give clothing? Why not?

WOMAN: Clothing – even things like ties – are too personal. Only good friends give them.

MAN: Huh? I never thought of a tie as being personal . . . just uncomfortable. What should you bring?

WOMAN: I don't know. Maybe something for the house.

NUMBER 3: *Switzerland*

MAN: We're meeting Mr. Mertz and his wife for dinner. Maybe I should bring flowers or something. . . . Yeah, I'll pick up some red roses.

WOMAN: You don't want to bring roses. In Switzerland, they could be a symbol of love and romance.

MAN: Oh, I didn't know that.

WOMAN: I think candy or chocolate might be better.

NUMBER 4: *Italy*

WOMAN: I'd like some flowers. Uh . . . those. About ten, I guess.

MAN: Ma'am, I don't think you should give ten flowers. In Italy, even numbers – 2, 4, 6, and so on – are bad luck.

WOMAN: Even numbers are bad luck? OK, I'll take nine flowers then.

NUMBER 5: JAPAN

[*Sound of store cash register; money exchanging*]

WOMAN: May I help you?

MAN: I'm going to stay with a family in Japan. I need to get something for them.

WOMAN: Pen sets are always a good gift.

MAN: Oh, that's a good idea. Let's see. . . . There are sets with a pen and pencil . . . and bigger sets with four pens.

WOMAN: You said you're going to Japan?

MAN: Yeah.

WOMAN: Don't give a set of four pens – in fact, don't give four of anything.

MAN: Why not?

WOMAN: The Japanese word for "four" sounds like the word for "death." It's bad luck.

MAN: Thanks for telling me. I'll take the pen and pencil set.

WOMAN: Good choice. These sets make very good gifts. After all, pens write in any language!

MAN: Uh . . . yeah. Right.

Page 41, Listening Task 2: Greetings around the world

Listen. There are many ways to greet people. These are a few examples from some countries.

Draw lines from the greetings to the places. Each has two answers.

NUMBER 1: A bow

MAN: Around the world, there are many different ways to greet people. Bowing is the traditional way of greeting in Northeast Asian countries like Korea and Japan. This picture, for example, shows how Japanese women bow. In Japan, when you bow, you don't look directly at the other person's eyes. But in Korea it's important to see the other person's face when you bow. In both countries, people bow to show respect.

NUMBER 2: A hug

MAN: When good friends meet in Russia, they often hug each other. This is true for both women and men. Russia isn't the only place where friends hug. In Brazil, for example, friends also hug each other in greeting. In Brazil, the hug is called an *abraço*.

NUMBER 3: The salaam

MAN: The *salaam* is a greeting from the Middle East. It is used in Jordan, Saudi Arabia, and some other Arab countries. It is most popular with older, more traditional people. To give a *salaam*, first touch your heart, then your forehead. Then your hand moves up, away from your head. When people use this greeting, they say, "Peace be with you."

NUMBER 4: The namaste or wai

MAN: People in India and in Thailand use a different kind of greeting. It is called *namaste* in India. In Thailand, it is call *wai*. The hands are put high on the chest. You bow slightly. It is a way of greeting, but it also means "Thank you" and "I'm sorry."

NUMBER 5: A strong, short handshake

MAN: You all know how to shake hands. This is common in many countries. But it isn't always done the same way. In the United States and Canada, for example, people usually give a strong, short handshake. It's short but rather firm.

NUMBER 6: A softer, longer handshake

MAN: In many other countries, people also shake hands. But they do it differently from in the U.S. and Canada. In Mexico and in Egypt, for example, many people – especially men – shake hands. Mexican and Egyptian handshakes usually last a little longer. The handshake is softer – not as strong.

Unit 13 Time changes everything.

Page 43, Listening Task 1: What did they use to do?

Listen. Did you guess the old jobs correctly? Correct your answers.

NUMBER 1: Arnold Schwarzenegger

WOMAN: Arnold Schwarzenegger wasn't always an actor. He used to be a bodybuilder. He won many bodybuilding contests.

NUMBER 2: Whoopi Goldberg

MAN: How about Whoopi Goldberg? She's a very funny actress now, but she used to be a schoolteacher. I wonder if she was a funny teacher.

NUMBER 3: Walt Disney

WOMAN: Do you know what Walt Disney's job was before he worked in movies? He was an ambulance driver. He drove an ambulance for the Red Cross in Europe.

NUMBER 4: Michelle Pfeiffer

MAN: Michelle Pfeiffer, the star of *Batman Returns,* worked as a store clerk when she was younger. The first time she was on TV, she played the part of a supermarket clerk.

NUMBER 5: Harrison Ford

WOMAN: Harrison Ford often acts the part of strong heroes. And he *is* strong. Before becoming a successful actor, he worked as a carpenter.

NUMBER 6: Bette Midler

MAN: Bette Midler is now a well-known actress. She's the star of many popular films. But what did she do before? She was a factory worker. She used to work in a pineapple factory.

NUMBER 7: Sean Connery

WOMAN: Sean Connery is a very famous actor. He's been in movies for over thirty-five years. He had many jobs before that. He was a porter for a while. In addition to being a porter, he also washed dishes and delivered milk to people's houses.

NUMBER 8: Cher

MAN: You probably know Cher as an actress. Did you know that she used to be a famous pop singer? During the 1960s, she was part of "Sonny and Cher," a popular music team.

NUMBER 9: Clint Eastwood

WOMAN: Today Clint Eastwood is famous for his action movies and westerns. When he was a college student, he worked at a gas station. He was a gas station attendant in Los Angeles.

Page 44, Listening Task 2: When I was younger . . .

Listen. What did you do use to do when you were a child? Write the missing words in the circles.

Then complete the sentences about yourself.

NUMBER 1

WOMAN: There are many ways for children to get to school. Some go on foot. Others go by car. Some go by bus or train. How did you use to get to elementary school?

MAN: When I was a child, I used to go to school [*xylophone tone*]
When I was a child, [*pause*] I used to go to school [*xylophone tone*]

NUMBER 2

MAN: People go many places during holidays. Some visit relatives like grandparents or aunts and uncles. Others go to the beach or the mountains. Others go swimming or shopping. When you were younger, where did you go during holidays?

WOMAN: During holidays, I used to go [*xylophone tone*]
During holidays, [pause] I used to go [*xylophone tone*]

NUMBER 3

WOMAN: What did you do after school when you were younger? Some children play with friends. Others go to club meetings. Some take extra classes or study. What did you do after school when you were younger?

MAN: After school, I used to [*xylophone tone*]
After school, [*pause*] I used to [*xylophone tone*]

NUMBER 4

MAN: Most children like games. Some play running games. Some play sports like soccer or baseball. What game did you play?

WOMAN: A game I used to play was [*xylophone tone*]
A game [*pause*] I used to play was [*xylophone tone*]

NUMBER 5

WOMAN: How about television? What TV shows were popular when you were younger? What was your favorite TV show?

MAN: My favorite TV show used to be [*xylophone tone*]
My favorite TV show [*pause*] used to be [*xylophone tone*]

NUMBER 6

MAN: Think about your hair ten years ago. Was your hair longer? Was it shorter? How about the style? Was it different when you were younger? How?

WOMAN: My hair used to be [*xylophone tone*]
My hair [*pause*] used to be [*xylophone tone*]

NUMBER 7

WOMAN: How about school? Were there things you didn't like about elementary school? Think of one thing you disliked.

MAN: At school I used to dislike [*xylophone tone*]
At school [*pause*] I used to dislike [*xylophone tone*]

NUMBER 8

MAN: What was your favorite season? Summer? Fall? Winter? Spring? Which season did you like the most?

WOMAN: The season I used to like the most was [*xylophone tone*]
The season [*pause*] I used to like the most was [*xylophone tone*]

Unit 14 Can you describe it?

Page 46, Listening Task I: Which one?

Listen. What are the people describing?
Check the correct pictures.
How did you know? Write the words.

NUMBER I

WOMAN: Well, it's a picture of a boy. He seems to be about eight years old, and he's pretty cute. He's fairly tall. I think he's been eating chocolate. The funny thing is that he's really dirty in this picture. His face is a mess!

NUMBER 2

WOMAN: I'd probably enjoy that book. It looks like a love story. I like books that . . . you know . . . make you feel warm and happy.

NUMBER 3

MAN: Actually, I don't like that one very much. It's too dark. I don't know . . . I think plain, dark clothes are boring.

NUMBER 4

MAN: Let's see. . . . There's a house in my picture. It's a strange old house . . . very narrow – tall and narrow. In front, there's a winding path. It just winds up the hill to the house.

NUMBER 5

WOMAN: Mysterious. He seems really mysterious. He's kind of ugly. Yeah, ugly and mysterious. I don't like him at all. He's scary.

NUMBER 6

MAN: Well, the woman seems to be very happy – like something good happened to her. She's smiling . . . well, maybe she's laughing.

Page 47, Listening Task 2: Your story

Listen to the story. Imagine the scene.

WOMAN: A road went through a forest. A woman was walking down the road. Suddenly she saw a man. He was wearing a shirt, pants, and a hat. He smiled and said something.

Listen again. Write the missing words on the lines. When you hear the bell, write any word in the circle that makes sense.

WOMAN: A [*sound of bell*] road went through a [*sound of bell*] forest. [*pause*]
A [*sound of bell*] road went through a [*sound of bell*] forest. [*pause*]

A [*sound of bell*] woman was walking down the road. [*pause*]
A [*sound of bell*] woman was walking down the road. [*pause*]

Suddenly she saw a [*sound of bell*] man. [*pause*]
Suddenly she saw a [*sound of bell*] man. [*pause*]

He was wearing a [*sound of bell*] shirt, [*pause*] [*sound of bell*] pants, [*pause*] and a [*sound of bell*] hat. [*pause*]

He was wearing a [*sound of bell*] shirt, [*pause*] [*sound of bell*] pants, [*pause*] and a [*sound of bell*] hat. [*pause*]

He smiled and said [*sound of bell*] [*pause*]
He smiled and said [*sound of bell*] [*pause*]

Unit 15 Languages

Page 49, Listening Task I: World languages

Listen. These are the eight languages with the most speakers.
Where do people speak them? Follow the instructions.

NUMBER I

WOMAN: There are more native speakers of Chinese than any other language. There are many types of Chinese. Two main types are

T20

Cantonese and Mandarin. Mandarin Chinese is the official language in China. More than 700 million people speak Mandarin Chinese. Find China and Taiwan in eastern Asia. Write a *C* for "Chinese" in the box.

NUMBER 2

MAN: More people speak English than any other language in the world. Many are native speakers. English is their first language. People speak English in the United States and most of Canada. Find the U.S. and Canada on the map. Write an *E* for "English" in the box.

WOMAN: People in the United Kingdom and Ireland speak English. The United Kingdom and Ireland are in western Europe. Find Ireland and the United Kingdom on the map. Write an *E* for "English" in the box.

Now find Australia and New Zealand. Australia and New Zealand are on the bottom right of the map. Write an *E* in the box.

MAN: Find India on the map. India is southwest of China. Write an *E* in one of the boxes. English is an official language in India. Some Indians speak English as a first language. Others use English as a *lingua franca*. That means a "common language." They use it to speak to people with different first languages.

NUMBER 3

WOMAN: Spanish is another major language. People in Spain and in Latin America speak Spanish. They speak it in Mexico, parts of the Caribbean, Central America, and South America. Find Mexico and South America on the map. Write an *S* for "Spanish" in the box. Do not write an *S* on Brazil. Brazil is not a Spanish-speaking country.

Now look at Europe. Find Spain. Write an *S* there, too.

NUMBER 4

MAN: There are many languages in India. Two important languages are Hindi and Bengali. Find India again. Write an *H* for "Hindi" and a *B* for "Bengali" in the other two boxes. That's *H* for "Hindi" and *B* for "Bengali."

NUMBER 5

WOMAN: People in northern Africa and in the Middle East speak Arabic. Egypt is in the middle of this area. Find Egypt on the map. Write an *A* for "Arabic" in the box.

NUMBER 6

MAN: Many people speak Russian. Russia is a big country. Find it on the map, above China. Write an *R* for "Russian" in the box.

NUMBER 7

WOMAN: Look at South America again. Find Brazil. Portuguese is the language of Brazil. Write a *P* for "Portuguese" in the box.

Now look at western Europe. Find Portugal. It's near Spain. Write a *P* in the box.

NUMBER 8

MAN: Most Japanese speakers are in Japan. Find eastern Asia. Japan is an island country. Write a *J* for "Japanese."

WOMAN: These are the eight languages in the world with the most speakers.

Page 50, Listening Task 2: Which English?

Look at the words. Can you tell the difference between American and British English?
Write *A* for "American."
Write *B* for "British."
Now listen to Chris and Helen. Chris is from the United States. Helen is from Great Britain. Correct your answers.

CHRIS: Hi. My name's Chris Paulsen. I'm from the United States. I live in Maryland.

HELEN: Hi. My name's Helen Forster. I'm British. I'm from Southampton in the south of England.

NUMBER 1

CHRIS: That? That's a truck, of course. I'd always call it a "truck."

HELEN: We wouldn't. To me, that's a lorry. We'd call it a "lorry."

CHRIS: "Truck" is American English.
HELEN: "Lorry" is British English.

NUMBER 2
HELEN: We have to tick our answers.
CHRIS: We have to what?
HELEN: Tick our answers. Like this.
CHRIS: Oh, check our answers. Put a check mark. I see.
HELEN: This mark is a "tick" in British English.
CHRIS: To Americans, it's a "check."

NUMBER 3
HELEN: I need to get a new cot for the baby.
CHRIS: A new what?
HELEN: A new cot – for the baby to sleep in.
CHRIS: Oh, a baby crib. We say "crib," not "cot."
HELEN: In British English, a baby's bed is a "cot."
CHRIS: In American English, it's a "crib."

NUMBER 4
CHRIS: I'm making eggplant for dinner.
HELEN: What's that?
CHRIS: Eggplant? You know. It's a black vegetable.
HELEN: Oh, you mean aubergine. Sorry I didn't understand. We say "aubergine."
CHRIS: This vegetable is an "eggplant" in America.
HELEN: In British English, it's an "aubergine."
Sometimes British and American pronunciation is different.

NUMBER 5
CHRIS: I'll recycle those aLUminum cans.
HELEN: Sorry? How did you say that?
CHRIS: Uh . . . aLUminum cans?
HELEN: That's interesting. We pronounce it aluMINium . . . aluMINium.
CHRIS: Really? Well, I'll recycle them . . . however we say it.
HELEN: In Britain, we stress the third syllable: MIN . . . alu<u>MIN</u>ium.

CHRIS: In American English, we stress LU . . . a<u>LU</u>minum.
HELEN: And the spelling is different, too. In British English, we spell it A-L-U-M-I-N-I-U-M – alu<u>MIN</u>ium.
CHRIS: In the United States, we spell it A-L-U-M-I-N-U-M – a<u>LU</u>minum.

NUMBER 6
HELEN: We've done them all – A to zed.
CHRIS: Is that how you say the last letter?
HELEN: Zed. Yes. Oh, you say "zee," right?
CHRIS: Yeah. W-X-Y-zee. . . . In the United States, we pronounce the last letter of the alphabet "zee."
HELEN: In British English, we say "zed." It's also "zed" in Canadian English, Australian English, Indian English . . . almost everywhere else.

Unit 16 I like that!

Page 52, Listening Task 1: Same or different?

Listen. What things does Sarah like? Check them.

NUMBER 1: Places to live
INTERVIEWER: Let's do this survey on preferences. Where do you prefer to live, Sarah? Do you like houses or apartments?
SARAH: Uh . . . apartments, I guess. They're not as much work to keep clean. Also, I like living downtown – near my job and near stores and restaurants. I think apartments are more convenient.

NUMBER 2: Food
INTERVIEWER: How about food? Which do you like best – beef, fish, or chicken?
SARAH: Well, I like them all, but I'd say I like chicken the best. It's healthy . . . and I know a lot of different ways to cook chicken.

NUMBER 3: TV
INTERVIEWER: The next question is about entertainment. Do you watch much TV?
SARAH: Not very much. I do watch the news

every day, though. I watch TV mainly for the news. I read more often than I watch TV.

NUMBER 4: Vacations

INTERVIEWER: How about vacations? Would you rather take a vacation in the mountains, at the beach, or in a big city?

SARAH: The mountains, definitely. I live in the city – which I like – but for vacation, I like to get away. I like to go camping, hiking . . . that sort of thing. So I like the mountains a lot.

NUMBER 5: School subjects

INTERVIEWER: One last question. When you were in school, what was your favorite subject?

SARAH: My favorite class in school? History. I like learning about important things, you know, events from the past. I like seeing what history tells us about life now.

Do you like the same things? Circle your answers.

Page 53, Listening Task 2: How about you?

Listen. What do you like to do? What don't you like to do?
Answer the questions with your own ideas.

NUMBER 1

WOMAN: Find the purple circle. Find the purple circle. What kind of food do you like to eat? What's your favorite food? Finish the sentence: I love . . .

MAN: Now find the green circle . . . the green circle. What food do you hate? What food do you really hate eating? Finish the sentence.

NUMBER 2

WOMAN: Find the purple triangle . . . the purple triangle. What musician – or kind of music – do you like to listen to? What musician – or kind of music – do you like? Finish the sentence.

MAN: Now find the green triangle. In the green triangle, finish the sentence. What kind of music – or what musician – don't you like? A musician or kind of music you do not like.

NUMBER 3

WOMAN: Look at the purple diamond . . . the purple diamond. What sport do you enjoy watching? What sport do you enjoy watching?

MAN: Now find the green diamond. In the green diamond, finish the sentence with a sport you dislike watching. A sport you dislike watching.

NUMBER 4

WOMAN: Now find the green square. In the green square, write a free-time activity you like to do. What do you like to do in your free time? Finish the sentence.

MAN: Finally, find the purple square . . . the purple square. What is a free-time activity you don't like to do? A free-time activity that you don't like to do. . . . Finish the sentence.

Unit 17 Strange news

Page 55, Listening Task 1: What . . . ?!

Listen. What are these stories about?
Write the newspaper headlines.

NUMBER 1

WOMAN: UFO sends TV sports show to earth.
MAN: UFO sends TV sports show to earth?

NUMBER 2

MAN: Giant kangaroos attack school.
WOMAN: Giant kangaroos attack school?

NUMBER 3

WOMAN: 2,000-year-old Greek statue has face of rock star.
MAN: 2,000-year-old Greek statue has face of rock star?

NUMBER 4

MAN: Man loses one hundred pounds.
WOMAN: Man loses one hundred pounds?

NUMBER 5

WOMAN: Elephant joins soccer team.
MAN: Elephant joins soccer team?

Page 56, Listening Task 2: Do you believe it?

Listen to these stories.
What information is in these stories? Check your answers.

NUMBER 1: UFO sends TV sports show to earth.

WOMAN: James Russell of Toronto had an unusual experience. He was watching television. Suddenly, the TV showed a strange picture. It was a sports game from space. The game seemed to take place on a UFO. The space creatures were playing with a ball of fire. Mr. Russell thinks the program was sent to earth from a UFO.

NUMBER 2: Giant kangaroos attack school.

MAN: Giant kangaroos from a national park near Canberra, Australia's capital, recently attacked an elementary school. The school was located on the edge of the city. A mob of about sixty kangaroos hopped through the school, smashing desks and breaking windows. Fortunately, the attack took place on a Sunday. No one was at school at the time, so no one was hurt. The kangaroos were much larger than most, about twice as tall as a man.

NUMBER 3: 2,000-year-old Greek statue has face of rock star.

WOMAN: Scientists in Greece found a statue that is over two thousand years old. The statue looks just like the famous rock-and-roll star Elvis Presley. How could the statue look like the American music star? The scientists say they don't know. Elvis's fans say it's proof he lived before.

NUMBER 4: Man loses one hundred pounds.

MAN: Roger Simms was overweight for years. His doctor told him to lose weight. If he didn't, he would get sick. Roger took the doctor's advice . . . too seriously, maybe. He lost one hundred pounds – that's nearly forty-five kilograms. How did he do it? By eating only watermelon. He ate watermelon for breakfast. Watermelon for lunch. And dinner? Watermelon. How does he feel now? Happy . . . and tired of eating watermelon.

NUMBER 5: Elephant joins soccer team.

WOMAN: The Blazers' soccer team has a new member – Zambo the elephant. The elephant has learned to kick the soccer ball. He can bounce the ball off his head. Of course, the elephant doesn't play in regular games. He performs tricks before the team's soccer matches. The kids love him. The players say Zambo is just like a member of the team.

Do you think these stories might be true? Draw lines to show your opinion.

Unit 18 Holidays

Page 58, Listening Task 1: Fireworks, food, and fun

Listen. People are talking about these holidays. When are they?
Write the numbers on the correct months. One item has two answers.

NUMBER 1: Martin Luther King Day

WOMAN: Martin Luther King Day is a holiday in the United States. The holiday is on January fifteenth, the birthday of Dr. Martin Luther King. On January fifteenth, people remember the things that Dr. King did to help all Americans have more freedom. In January, it is still very cold, so people usually celebrate this holiday indoors. Famous people often give speeches at schools and community centers.

NUMBER 2: Moon Festival

MAN: The Moon Festival is a Chinese holiday. The holiday is in September or October. The dates change, based on the traditional Chinese calendar. The Moon Festival is a day for people to give thanks for the good things that happened during the year. On this holiday, people eat cakes that are round like the moon. The Moon Festival is also a time for families to get together. The Moon Festival takes place right before the harvest in September or October. People celebrate because most of the hard work in the fields is now finished.

NUMBER 3: St. Patrick's Day

WOMAN: St. Patrick's Day is March seventeenth. It is named for a man who lived in Ireland. Of course, Irish people celebrate the day, but it's an even bigger festival in the United States. People – especially Irish-Americans – wear green on St. Patrick's Day. In Chicago, they even make the river green. People also have parties, and in large cities like New York and Chicago, there are big parades.

NUMBER 4: Thanksgiving (The United States)

MAN: People in North America celebrate Thanksgiving in the fall. In the United States, Thanksgiving is the fourth Thursday in November. People give thanks for the good things in their lives. Families get together. There is always a big meal. Turkey is the most popular main dish. There are many other kinds of food, too, including potatoes and other vegetables, and pumpkin pie.

NUMBER 5: Thanksgiving (Canada)

WOMAN: In Canada, Thanksgiving is in October – the second Monday in October. Canadian Thanksgiving is also a time for families to gather for a big dinner. People give thanks for the good food and for the other good things in their lives.

NUMBER 6: Day of the Dead

MAN: The Day of the Dead is a very important holiday in Mexico. This is the day that the dead come back to visit their families. The Day of the Dead is November first. People go to visit the graves of people who have died. They have picnics near these graves and bring food and flowers for the dead. November first, the Day of the Dead, is a time for remembering.

NUMBER 7: St. Lucia's Day

WOMAN: St. Lucia's Day is a holiday in Sweden. It is in December. St. Lucia's Day is a day to bring light into the house. Little girls wear white dresses and carry tree greens. In December, towns all over Sweden choose their Queen of Light. Homes and shops all burn candles throughout the day. People also eat buns. These buns are for good luck.

NUMBER 8: Independence Day

MAN: The Fourth of July is American Independence Day. It is the birthday of the United States. July fourth is celebrated with parades and picnics during the day. Most people don't have to work. They go outside and enjoy the summer weather. People eat hot dogs and hamburgers. Sometimes they go to baseball games. In the evening, everyone gathers to enjoy the fireworks. They are very colorful and light up the sky for miles.

NUMBER 9: Children's Day

WOMAN: Children's Day is a Japanese festival that is celebrated in May. Outside their homes, families with boys fly brightly colored flags that look like fish. In the past, this festival was just "Boys' Day." Now families honor both boys and girls on this day. May fifth is a national holiday in Japan.

Page 59, Listening Task 2: Good times

Listen. You will hear about holidays around the world.

Number the pictures (1–4).

Write one more thing about each holiday.

NUMBER 1

WOMAN: Kite flying is popular in many countries. It has a special meaning in Korea. In the first half of January, many Korean boys fly kites. On January 15th, they write "No bad luck" on their kites. They fly them very high in the sky. Then they cut the string. The kite flies away. It takes the bad luck away for the year.

NUMBER 2

MAN: Many countries have holidays to bring good luck. In Thailand, they hold a water festival. The festival takes place everywhere in Thailand, but it is especially popular in the north. The water festival takes place in the middle of April. People throw buckets of water on each other. There are even parades where people throw water. It's especially important to pour water on older people. It shows respect.

NUMBER 3

MAN: Brazil is famous for its huge festival, with lots of music and dancing. The festival is called "Carnival." The most famous Carnival parties are in Rio de Janeiro. In Rio, bands travel through the streets in parades. People enjoy dancing and dressing up in fancy clothes. It's a time of year to have a good time. The American festival of Mardi Gras, in New Orleans, is similar to Carnival.

NUMBER 4

WOMAN: Chinese New Year is usually a four-day holiday. Chinese communities all over the world celebrate this holiday. It is a happy time in the Chinese calendar, and the four days of Chinese New Year are very noisy. There are parades in the streets, and families gather for big dinners. At these dinners, children get "lucky money" in red envelopes. Before the New Year, Chinese people always clean their houses to clean out bad luck. Everything must be fresh and clean. People also make sure they have paid all their bills. It is important to start the New Year without owing anyone money.

Unit 19 Inventions

Page 61, Listening Task 1: Where in the world?

Listen. Were your guesses right?
Correct your answers.
Write one more fact about each invention.

NUMBER 1

WOMAN: People in England made the first computer. It was built in 1943. It was made to help England understand secret messages during World War II.

NUMBER 2

MAN: Someone in Australia invented the fax machine. After the fax machine was invented, it first became popular in East Asia.

NUMBER 3

WOMAN: Folding fans came from Japan. They were invented in Japan almost 800 years ago.

NUMBER 4

MAN: The first car came from Germany. It was invented by Karl Benz in 1885. Benz is still famous. His name is on the Mercedes-Benz car.

NUMBER 5

WOMAN: A man in Canada invented the chocolate bar. He lived in Nova Scotia – in the eastern part of Canada. He invented the chocolate bar in the 1800s.

NUMBER 6

MAN: The first really accurate calendar was invented in Mexico. This calendar was made about fifteen hundred years ago. That's when people learned that the year was three hundred and sixty-five days long.

NUMBER 7

WOMAN: The first mechanical clock was invented in China. It was invented in the year 725 – over one thousand two hundred and fifty years ago.

NUMBER 8

MAN: People think Africans created the first puppets. Actually, no one is sure, but puppets were probably created to help tell stories.

Page 62, Listening Task 2: That's really strange!

Listen. These are real products.
What are they used for? Write your answers.

NUMBER 1

[*Sound of store noises*]

MAN: Good afternoon. May I help you?

WOMAN: Yeah. I'm going camping, and I need something to keep the insects away.

MAN: How about these? They're new. They're insect guards.

WOMAN: I've never seen anything like them.

MAN: You can use them to keep insects off you – flies, mosquitoes . . . any insect.

WOMAN: These will keep insects off me? How?

MAN: They cover you. You know, like a net. You put one on your head, one on each hand, and one on each foot. You just put them over your body. The insects can't bite you.

WOMAN: Right. Actually, I think I just want some insect spray.

MAN: You don't want to try the guards?

WOMAN: No, thanks. Just a can of insect spray, please.

MAN: I see.

NUMBER 2

MAN: What's this?

WOMAN: Oh, I just bought it. It's an electric spaghetti fork.

MAN: An electric spaghetti fork?

WOMAN: Yeah. You can use it to eat spaghetti.

MAN: I don't understand.

WOMAN: You put it in the spaghetti. Then you turn it on. [*sound of buzzing motor*] The fork moves in a circle. It pulls the spaghetti around the fork.

MAN: Does this really help you to eat spaghetti?

WOMAN: Well, um . . . I haven't tried it yet. I just bought it. But it looked interesting.

MAN: Better living through technology.

NUMBER 3

[*Sound of pet store noises*]

WOMAN: OK, you've got cat food and a brush. Anything else for your cat?

MAN: I don't think so.

WOMAN: Have you seen our new cat mop?

MAN: Uh . . . no.

WOMAN: Oh, it's the cutest thing. You can use it to have your cat clean the floor.

MAN: I don't think my cat *wants* to clean the floor.

WOMAN: Oh, he doesn't have a choice. You put these shoes on the cat. On the bottom of each one, there's a little mop. As the cat runs, it cleans the floor.

MAN: I can use it to have my cat clean the floor? I don't think so.

WOMAN: I think they're going to be very popular.

MAN: Do cats like them?

WOMAN: Well, I think so. I haven't actually tried them out . . . on a cat . . .

NUMBER 4

WOMAN: Look what I made!

MAN: It looks like a child's swing . . . but with hooks. What's it for?

WOMAN: You know how crowded the subway is in the morning?

MAN: Yeah.

WOMAN: Well, you can use this to sit down on the train.

MAN: Use it to sit down on the train? I don't understand.

WOMAN: When you can't find a seat, you just put the hooks over those bars on top of the train.

MAN: I don't get it.

WOMAN: When there are no seats on the train, you can sit down on this. Put the hooks over the bars. It makes a little seat.

MAN: You've been working really hard lately, haven't you?

NUMBER 5

MAN: Do you want to see something?

WOMAN: Sure. What?

MAN: Look.

WOMAN: What is it?

MAN: It's an electric letter opener.

WOMAN: A what?

MAN: An electric letter opener. I can use it to open letters. Watch. I put the letter in here . . . [*sound of motorized buzzing*]

WOMAN: You use it to open letters?
MAN: Yeah. It only takes about two seconds.
WOMAN: Uh . . . how long does it take you with a knife?
MAN: Yeah, but it's electric.

Would you want these items? Which ones? Circle them.

Unit 20 Folktales

Page 64, Listening Task 1: The farmer and his sons

Listen. You will hear a traditional folktale. Number the pictures (1–6).

WOMAN: Once upon a time, a farmer and his three sons lived on a farm. The farmer worked very hard in his fields. But his sons did not like to work. They were very lazy and only wanted to have a good time. [*pause*]
   One day, the farmer called his sons to him. He said,
FATHER: Sons, I am old. I will soon die. I'm leaving you a treasure in the fields. There's a treasure in the fields.
FIRST SON: A treasure? Is it money?
SECOND SON: Gold?
THIRD SON: Diamonds?
FATHER: A treasure. You will find a treasure in the fields. [*pause*]
WOMAN: The old farmer died. His sons ran to the fields. They began digging and digging. Soon, they dug up the whole field. But they found no treasure. [*pause*]
   The field was already dug for planting, so they decided to plant some wheat. The wheat grew and grew. They sold the wheat, and they made a lot of money. [*pause*]
   But the sons still wanted to find the treasure, so they dug up the field again. Once again, they found no treasure, so once again they planted wheat. They did this year after year. [*pause*]
   After many years, the sons began to enjoy working hard on their farm. They had good lives. And they finally understood: The *land* was their father's treasure. The land itself brought them a good life. [*pause*]

Page 65, Listening Task 2: The medicine pipe

This story is from North America. The medicine pipe is important for many Native Americans. It was a gift from their god, the Great Maker of All Things.
Listen to the story of the pipe. These words will help you.

MAN: It was a winter night, hundreds of years ago. It was very cold. Snow covered the earth. Two young men walked through the snow. The young men were lost. They didn't know where they were. They were very hungry. Suddenly something moved. By the light of the moon, they could see that it was a woman – a beautiful, young woman. A woman, carrying a bundle of food.
One of the men ran toward her. He was going to steal her food. Just before he reached her, he fell. He fell to the ground. He stopped breathing. The man was dead.
The other man watched silently. The woman looked at him. She smiled. She put the food on the ground. She pointed to the food and smiled again. He took the food and ate until he was full.
Then the woman sat on the ground. Her body began to change. She changed into a buffalo. A buffalo – the gift of the Great Maker. Then the buffalo began to change. It changed – into a medicine pipe.
The young man walked to the pipe. He picked it up. He held it carefully. The young man found his way back to camp. He gave the pipe to his people. They knew it was a gift from the Great Maker of All Things. The Great Maker would always be with them.

Did you like this story? Do you know a story like it?

A Listening and Speaking Game

Activation is a review game. The questions and tasks are designed to encourage students to use the forms, functions, and topics they've heard throughout *Active Listening*.

1. Divide the class into groups of four. T: *Work in groups of four.*

2. Hold your book so that students can see the game on pages 66 and 67. T: *Each group uses one book. Open the book to pages 66 and 67. Put the book on the table.*

3. T: *Each person needs a place marker – a coin, an eraser, or any small object. Put the marker on the "Start here" square.*

4. Point to the "How many spaces?" box on page 67. T: *One person, close your eyes. Touch the "How many spaces?" box with a pencil.*

5. T: *Move that many spaces. Read the sentence or sentences. Answer with at least three things.*

6. T: *Now each partner asks one question about what the first player said.*

7. T: *Continue playing. Take turns.*

8. Allow adequate time for students to play.

NOTES

• Although *Activation* reviews language from the entire syllabus, you may wish to have students play it before they have finished the book.

• With activities that have several steps, sometimes giving instructions can be difficult, particularly in large classes. It is usually better to demonstrate. Divide the class into groups. Direct one group through the game as one member from each of the other groups watches. Those members then return to their own groups and teach the other players what to do.

• Many students often enjoy playing the game more than once. If they change partners each time they play, the information will remain new.

• As students play, encourage partners to ask questions about each other's answers. The questions can be either to clarify things not understood or to expand on interesting information.

• If there is a question someone doesn't want to answer, allow any other player to ask a different question.

• *Activation* is best used as a cooperative game. It isn't necessary to give points. However, if you feel your students need the extra support of competition, you can give one point for each sentence a student says while answering each item.

• Because this is a fluency game, corrections are usually not appropriate while the students play.